AUTOBIOGRAPHY

OF AN

ASPIRING SAINT

THE
OTHER VOICE
IN
EARLY MODERN
EUROPE

Series Editors
Margaret L. King and
Albert Rabil, Jr.

Cecilia Ferrazzi

AUTOBIOGRAPHY
OF AN
ASPIRING SAINT

ঌ

Transcribed, Translated, and Edited
by
Anne Jacobson Schutte

THE UNIVERSITY OF CHICAGO PRESS
Chicago & London

Anne Jacobson Schutte is professor of history at the University of Virginia.

The University of Chicago Press, Chicago 60637
The University of Chicago Press, Ltd., London
© 1996 by The University of Chicago
All rights reserved. Published 1996
Printed in the United States of America
05 04 03 02 01   5 4 3 2

ISBN (cloth): 0-226-24446-6
ISBN (paper): 0-226-24447-4

Library of Congress Cataloging-in-Publication Data
Ferrazzi, Cecilia, 1609–1684.
    [Autobiografia di una santa mancata. English]
    Autobiography of an aspiring saint / Cecilia Ferrazzi ;
transcribed, translated, and edited by Anne Jacobson Schutte.
        p.   cm.—(The other voice in early modern Europe)
    Includes bibliographical references and index.
    ISBN 0-226-24446-6.—ISBN 0-226-24447-4 (pbk.).
    1. Ferrazzi, Cecilia, 1609–1684. 2.Catholics—Italy—Venice—
Biography. 3. Women—Italy—Venice—Biography. 4. Inquisition—
Italy—Venice—History—17th century—Sources. 5. Venice (Italy)—
Biography. I. Schutte, Anne Jacobson. II. Title III. Series.
BX4705.F48A3   1996b
282'.092—dc20   96-24316
    [B]   CIP

For Natalie Zemon Davis,
with gratitude and affection

CONTENTS

INTRODUCTION
TO THE SERIES

Margaret L. King and Albert Rabil, Jr.

THE OLD VOICE AND THE OTHER VOICE

In western Europe and the United States women are nearing equality in the professions, in business, and in politics. Most enjoy access to education, reproductive rights, and autonomy in financial affairs. Issues vital to women are on the public agenda: equal pay, child care, domestic abuse, breast cancer research, and curricular revision with an eye to the inclusion of women.

These recent achievements have their origins in things women (and some male supporters) said for the first time about six hundred years ago. Theirs is the "other voice," in contradistinction to the "first voice," the voice of the educated men who created western culture. Coincident with a general reshaping of European culture in the period 1300 to 1700 (called the Renaissance or Early Modern period), questions of female equality and opportunity were raised that still resound and are still unresolved.

The "other voice" emerged against the backdrop of a 3,000-year history of misogyny—the hatred of women—rooted in the civilizations related to western culture: Hebrew, Greek, Roman, and Christian. Misogyny inherited from these traditions pervaded the intellectual, medical, legal, religious and social systems that developed during the European Middle Ages.

The following pages describe the misogynistic tradition inherited by early modern Europeans, and the new tradition which the "other voice" called into being to challenge its assumptions. This review should serve as a framework for the understanding of the texts published in the series "The Other Voice in Early Modern Europe." Introductions specific to each text and author follow this essay in all the volumes of the series.

THE MISOGYNIST TRADITION, 500 BCE–1500 CE

Embedded in the philosophical and medical theories of the ancient Greeks were perceptions of the female as inferior to the male in both mind and body. Similarly, the structure of civil legislation inherited from the ancient Romans was biased against women, and the views on women developed by Christian thinkers out of the Hebrew Bible and the Christian New Testament were negative and disabling. Literary works composed in the vernacular language of ordinary people, and widely recited or read, conveyed these negative assumptions. The social networks within which most women lived—those of the family and the institutions of the Roman Catholic church—were shaped by this misogynist tradition and sharply limited the areas in which women might act in and upon the world.

GREEK PHILOSOPHY AND FEMALE NATURE Greek biology assumed that women were inferior to men and defined them merely as child-bearers and housekeepers. This view was authoritatively expressed in the works of the philosopher Aristotle.

Aristotle thought in dualities. He considered action superior to inaction, form (the inner design or structure of any object) superior to matter, completion to incompletion, possession to deprivation. In each of these dualities, he associated the male principle with the superior quality and the female with the inferior. "The male principle in nature," he argued, "is associated with active, formative and perfected characteristics, while the female is passive, material and deprived, desiring the male in order to become complete."[1] Men are always identified with virile qualities, such as judgment, courage and stamina; women with their opposites—irrationality, cowardice, and weakness.

Even in the womb, the masculine principle was considered superior. Man's semen, Aristotle believed, created the form of a new human creature, while the female body contributed only matter. (The existence of the ovum, and the other facts of human embryology, were not established until the seventeenth century.) Although the later Greek physician Galen believed that there was a female component in generation, contributed by "female semen," the followers of both Aristotle and Galen saw the male role in human generation as more active and more important.

In the Aristotelian view, the male principle sought always to reproduce itself. The creation of a female was always a mistake, therefore, resulting

---

1. Aristotle, *Physics*, 1.9 192a20–24 (*The Complete Works of Aristotle*, ed. Jonathan Barnes, rev. Oxford translation, 2 vols. [Princeton, N.J.: Princeton University Press, 1984], 1:328).

from an imperfect act of generation. Every female born was considered a "defective" or "mutilated" male (as Aristotle's terminology has variously been translated), a "monstrosity" of nature.[2]

For Greek theorists, the biology of males and females was the key to their psychology. The female was softer and more docile, more apt to be despondent, querulous, and deceitful. Being incomplete, moreover, she craved sexual fulfillment in intercourse with a male. The male was intellectual, active, and in control of his passions.

These psychological polarities derived from the theory that the universe consisted of four elements (earth, fire, air and water), expressed in human bodies as four "humors" (black bile, yellow bile, blood, and phlegm) considered respectively dry, hot, damp, and cold, and corresponding to mental states ("melancholic," "choleric," "sanguine," "phlegmatic"). In this schematization, the male, sharing the principles of earth and fire, was dry and hot; the female, sharing the principles of air and water, was cold and damp.

Female psychology was further affected by her dominant organ, the uterus (womb), *hystera* in Greek. The passions generated by the womb made women lustful, deceitful, talkative, irrational, indeed—when these affects were in excess—"hysterical."

Aristotle's biology also had social and political consequences. If the male principle was superior and the female inferior, then in the household, as in the state, men should rule and women must be subordinate. That hierarchy does not rule out the companionship of husband and wife, whose cooperation was necessary for the welfare of children and the preservation of property. Such mutuality supported male preeminence.

Aristotle's teacher Plato suggested a different possibility: that men and women might possess the same virtues. The setting for this proposal is the imaginary and ideal Republic that Plato sketches in a dialogue of that name. Here, for a privileged elite capable of leading wisely, all distinctions of class and wealth dissolve, as do consequently those of gender. Without households or property, as Plato constructs his ideal society, there is no need for the subordination of women. Women may, therefore, be educated to the same level as men to assume leadership responsibilities. Plato's Republic remained imaginary, however. In real societies, the subordination of women remained the norm and the prescription.

The views of women inherited from the Greek philosophical tradition became the basis for medieval thought. In the thirteenth century, the su-

2. Aristotle, *Generation of Animals*, 2.3 737a27–28 (ibid., 1:1144).

preme scholastic philosopher Thomas Aquinas, among others, still echoed Aristotle's views of human reproduction, of male and female personalities, and of the preeminent male role in the social hierarchy.

ROMAN LAW AND THE FEMALE CONDITION Roman law, like Greek philosophy, underlay medieval thought and shaped medieval society. The ancient belief that adult, property-owning men should administer households and make decisions affecting the community at large is the very fulcrum of Roman law.

Around 450 BCE, during Rome's republican era, the community's customary law was recorded (legendarily) on Twelve Tables erected in the city's central forum. It was later elaborated by professional jurists whose activity increased in the imperial era, when much new legislation, especially on issues affecting family and inheritance, was passed. This growing, changing body of laws was eventually codified in the *Corpus of Civil Law* under the direction of the Emperor Justinian, generations after the empire ceased to be ruled from Rome. That *Corpus*, read and commented upon by medieval scholars from the eleventh century on, inspired the legal systems of most of the cities and kingdoms of Europe.

Laws regarding dowries, divorce, and inheritance most pertain to women. Since those laws aimed to maintain and preserve property, the women concerned were those from the property-owning minority. Their subordination to male family members points to the even greater subordination of lower-class and slave women about whom the laws speak little.

In the early Republic, the *paterfamilias*, "father of the family," possessed *patria potestas*, "paternal power." The term *pater*, "father," in both these cases does not necessarily mean biological father, but householder. The father was the person who owned the household's property and, indeed, its human members. The *paterfamilias* had absolute power—including the power, rarely exercised, of life or death—over his wife, his children, and his slaves, as much as over his cattle.

Children could be "emancipated," an act that granted legal autonomy and the right to own property. Male children over the age of fourteen could be emancipated by a special grant from the father, or automatically by their father's death. But females never could be emancipated; instead, they passed from the authority of their father to a husband or, if widowed or orphaned while still unmarried, to a guardian or tutor.

Marriage under its traditional form placed the woman under her husband's authority, or *manus*. He could divorce her on grounds of adultery, drinking wine, or stealing from the household, but she could not divorce him. She could possess no property in her own right, nor bequeath any to her children upon her death. When her husband died, the household property passed not to her but to his male heirs. And when her father died, she had no claim to any family inheritance, which was directed to her brothers or more remote male relatives. The effect of these laws was to exclude women from civil society, itself based on property ownership.

In the later Republican and Imperial periods, these rules were significantly modified. Women rarely married according to the traditional form, but according to the form of "free" marriage. That practice allowed a woman to remain under her father's authority, to possess property given her by her father (most frequently the "dowry," recoverable from the husband's household in the event of his death), and to inherit from her father. She could also bequeath property to her own children and divorce her husband, just as he could divorce her.

Despite this greater freedom, women still suffered enormous disability under Roman law. Heirs could belong only to the father's side, never the mother's. Moreover, although she could bequeath her property to her children, she could not establish a line of succession in doing so. A woman was "the beginning and end of her own family," growled the jurist Ulpian. Moreover, women could play no public role. They could not hold public office, represent anyone in a legal case, or even witness a will. Women had only a private existence, and no public personality.

The dowry system, the guardian, women's limited ability to transmit wealth, and total political disability are all features of Roman law adopted, although modified according to local customary laws, by the medieval communities of western Europe.

CHRISTIAN DOCTRINE AND WOMEN'S PLACE The Hebrew Bible and the Christian New Testament authorized later writers to limit women to the realm of the family and to burden them with the guilt of original sin. The passages most fruitful for this purpose were the creation narratives in Genesis and sentences from the Epistles defining women's role within the Christian family and community.

Each of the first two chapters of Genesis contains a creation narrative. In the first "God created man in his own image, in the image of God he created him; male and female he created them." (NRSV, Genesis 1:27) In the second, God created Eve from Adam's rib (2:21–23). Christian theologians relied principally on Genesis 2 for their understanding of the relation between man and woman, interpreting the creation of Eve from Adam as proof of her subordination to him.

The creation story in Genesis 2 leads to that of the temptations in Genesis 3: of Eve by the wily serpent, and of Adam by Eve. As read by Christian theologians from Tertullian to Thomas Aquinas, the narrative made Eve responsible for the Fall and its consequences. She instigated the act; she deceived her husband; she suffered the greater punishment. Her disobedience made it necessary for Jesus to be incarnated and to die on the cross. From the pulpit, moralists and preachers for centuries conveyed to women the guilt that they bore for original sin.

The Epistles offered advice to early Christians on building communities of the faithful. Among the matters to be regulated was the place of women. Paul offered views favorable to women in Galatians 3:28: "There is neither Jew nor Greek, there is neither slave nor free, there is neither male nor female; for you are all one in Christ Jesus." Paul also referred to women as his co-workers and placed them on a par with himself and his male co-workers (Phil. 4:2–3; Rom. 16:1–3; I Cor. 16:19). Elsewhere Paul limited women's possibilities: "But I want you to understand that the head of every man is Christ, the head of a woman is her husband, and the head of Christ is God." (I Cor. 11:3)

Biblical passages by later writers (though attributed to Paul) enjoined women to forego jewels, expensive clothes, and elaborate coiffures; and they forbade women to "teach or have authority over men," telling them to "learn in silence with all submissiveness" as is proper for one responsible for sin, consoling them however with the thought that they will be saved through childbearing (I Tim. 2:9–15). Other texts among the later epistles defined women as the weaker sex, and emphasized their subordination to their husbands (I Peter 3:7; Col. 3:18; Eph. 5:22–23).

These passages from the New Testament became the arsenal employed by theologians of the early church to transmit negative attitudes toward women to medieval Christian culture—above all, Tertullian ("On the Apparel of Women"), Jerome (*Against Jovinian*), and Augustine (*The Literal Meaning of Genesis*).

THE IMAGE OF WOMEN IN MEDIEVAL LITERATURE The philosophical, legal and religious traditions born in antiquity formed the basis of the medieval intellectual synthesis wrought by trained thinkers, mostly clerics, writing in Latin and based largely in universities. The vernacular literary tradition which developed alongside the learned tradition also spoke about female nature and women's roles. Medieval stories, poems, and epics were also infused with misogyny. They portrayed most women as lustful and deceitful, while praising good housekeepers and loyal wives, or replicas of the Virgin Mary, or the female saints and martyrs.

There is an exception in the movement of "courtly love" that evolved in southern France from the twelfth century. Courtly love was the erotic love between a nobleman and noblewoman, the latter usually superior in

social rank. It was always adulterous. From the conventions of courtly love
derive modern western notions of romantic love. The phenomenon has had
an impact disproportionate to its size, for it affected only a tiny elite, and
very few women. The exaltation of the female lover probably does not re-
flect a higher evaluation of women, or a step toward their sexual liberation.
More likely it gives expression to the social and sexual tensions besetting
the knightly class at a specific historical juncture.

The literary fashion of courtly love was on the wane by the thirteenth
century, when the widely read *Romance of the Rose* was composed in French
by two authors of significantly different dispositions. Guillaume de Lorris
composed the initial 4,000 verses around 1235, and Jean de Meun added
about 17,000 verses—more than four times the original—around 1265.

The fragment composed by Guillaume de Lorris stands squarely in the
courtly love tradition. Here the poet, in a dream, is admitted into a walled
garden where he finds a magic fountain in which a rosebush is reflected. He
longs to pick one rose but the thorns around it prevent his doing so, even
as he is wounded by arrows from the God of Love, whose commands he
agrees to obey. The remainder of this part of the poem recounts the poet's
unsuccessful efforts to pluck the rose.

The longer part of the *Romance* by Jean de Meun also describes a dream.
But here allegorical characters give long didactic speeches, providing a
social satire on a variety of themes, including those pertaining to women.
Love is an anxious and tormented state, the poem explains, women are
greedy and manipulative, marriage is miserable, beautiful women are lustful,
ugly ones cease to please, and a chaste woman, as rare as a black swan, can
scarcely be found.

Shortly after Jean de Meun completed *The Romance of the Rose*, Mathéolus
penned his *Lamentations*, a long Latin diatribe against marriage translated into
French about a century later. The *Lamentations* sum up medieval attitudes
toward women and provoked the important response by Christine de Pizan
in her *Book of the City of Ladies*.

In 1355, Giovanni Boccaccio wrote *Il Corbaccio*, another antifeminist
manifesto, though ironically by an author whose other works pioneered
new directions in Renaissance thought. The former husband of his lover
appears to Boccaccio, condemning his unmoderated lust and detailing the
defects of women. Boccaccio concedes at the end "how much men naturally
surpass women in nobility"[3] and is cured of his desires.

WOMEN'S ROLES: THE FAMILY The negative perception of women ex-

---

3. Giovanni Boccaccio, *The Corbaccio or The Labyrinth of Love*, trans. and ed. Anthony K. Cassell
(rev. paper ed.; Binghamton, N.Y.: Medieval and Renaissance Texts and Studies, 1993), 71.

pressed in the intellectual tradition are also implicit in the actual roles that women played in European society. Assigned to subordinate positions in the household and the church, they were barred from significant participation in public life.

Medieval European households, like those in antiquity and in nonwestern civilizations, were headed by males. It was the male serf, or peasant, feudal lord, town merchant, or citizen who was polled or taxed or succeeded to an inheritance or had any acknowledged public role, although their wives or widows could stand on a temporary basis as surrogates for them. From about 1100, the position of property-holding males was enhanced further. Inheritance was confined to the male, or agnate, line—with depressing consequences for women.

A wife never fully belonged to her husband's family or a daughter to her father's family. She left her father's house young to marry whomever her parents chose. Her dowry was managed by her husband and normally passed to her children by him at her death.

A married woman's life was occupied nearly constantly with cycles of pregnancy, childbearing, and lactation. Women bore children through all the years of their fertility, and many died in childbirth before the end of that term. They also bore responsibility for raising young children up to six or seven. That responsibility was shared in the propertied classes, since it was common for a wet-nurse to take over the job of breastfeeding, and servants took over other chores.

Women trained their daughters in the household responsibilities appropriate to their status, nearly always in tasks associated with textiles: spinning, weaving, sewing, embroidering. Their sons were sent out of the house as apprentices or students, or their training was assumed by fathers in later childhood and adolescence. On the death of her husband, a woman's children became the responsibility of his family. She generally did not take "his" children with her to a new marriage or back to her father's house, except sometimes in artisan classes.

Women also worked. Rural peasants performed farm chores, merchant wives often practiced their husband's trade, the unmarried daughters of the urban poor worked as servants or prostitutes. All wives produced or embellished textiles and did the housekeeping, while wealthy ones managed servants. These labors were unpaid or poorly paid, but often contributed substantially to family wealth.

WOMEN'S ROLES: THE CHURCH Membership in a household, whether a father's or a husband's, meant for women a lifelong subordination to others. In western Europe, the Roman Catholic church offered an alternative to the career of wife and mother. A woman could enter a convent parallel in function to the monasteries for men that evolved in the early Christian centuries.

In the convent, a woman pledged herself to a celibate life, lived according to strict community rules, and worshipped daily. Often the convent offered training in Latin, allowing some women to become considerable scholars and authors, as well as scribes, artists, and musicians. For women who chose the conventual life, the benefits could be enormous, but for numerous others placed in convents by paternal choice, the life could be restrictive and burdensome.

The conventual life declined as an alternative for women as the modern age approached. Reformed monastic institutions resisted responsibility for related female orders. The church increasingly restricted female institutional life by insisting on closer male supervision.

Women often sought other options. Some joined the communities of laywomen that sprang up spontaneously in the thirteenth century in the urban zones of western Europe, especially in Flanders and Italy. Some joined the heretical movements that flourished in late medieval Christendom, whose anticlerical and often antifamily positions particularly appealed to women. In these communities, some women were acclaimed as "holy women" or "saints," while others often were condemned as frauds or heretics.

In all, though the options offered to women by the church were sometimes less than satisfactory, sometimes they were richly rewarding. After 1520, the convent remained an option only in Roman Catholic territories. Protestantism engendered an ideal of marriage as a heroic endeavor, and appeared to place husband and wife on a more equal footing. Sermons and treatises, however, still called for female subordination and obedience.

THE OTHER VOICE, 1300–1700

Misogyny was so long-established in European culture when the modern era opened that to dismantle it was a monumental labor. The process began as part of a larger cultural movement that entailed the critical reexamination of ideas inherited from the ancient and medieval past. The humanists launched that critical reexamination.

THE HUMANIST FOUNDATION Originating in Italy in the fourteenth century, humanism quickly became the dominant intellectual movement in Europe. Spreading in the sixteenth century from Italy to the rest of Europe, it fueled the literary, scientific and philosophical movements of the era, and laid the basis for the eighteenth-century Enlightenment.

Humanists regarded the scholastic philosophy of medieval universities as out of touch with the realities of urban life. They found in the rhetorical discourse of classical Rome a language adapted to civic life and public speech. They learned to read, speak, and write classical Latin, and eventually classical Greek. They founded schools to teach others to do so, establishing the pattern for elementary and secondary education for the next three hundred years.

In the service of complex government bureaucracies, humanists employed their skills to write eloquent letters, deliver public orations, and formulate public policy. They developed new scripts for copying manuscripts and used the new printing press for the dissemination of texts, for which they created methods of critical editing.

Humanism was a movement led by males who accepted the evaluation of women in ancient texts and generally shared the misogynist perceptions of their culture. (Female humanists, as will be seen, did not.) Yet humanism also opened the door to the critique of the misogynist tradition. By calling authors, texts, and ideas into question, it made possible the fundamental rereading of the whole intellectual tradition that was required in order to free women from cultural prejudice and social subordination.

A DIFFERENT CITY The other voice first appeared when, after so many centuries, the accumulation of misogynist concepts evoked a response from a capable woman female defender: Christine de Pizan. Introducing her *Book of the City of Ladies* (1405), she described how she was affected by reading Mathéolus's *Lamentations:* "Just the sight of this book . . . made me wonder how it happened that so many different men . . . are so inclined to express both in speaking and in their treatises and writings so many wicked insults about women and their behavior."[4] These statements impelled her to detest herself "and the entire feminine sex, as though we were monstrosities in nature."[5]

The remainder of the *Book of the City of Ladies* presents a justification of the female sex and a vision of an ideal community of women. A pioneer, she has not only received the misogynist message, but she rejects it. From the fourteenth to seventeenth century, a huge body of literature accumulated that responded to the dominant tradition.

4. Christine de Pizan, *The Book of the City of Ladies*, trans. Earl Jeffrey Richards; Foreword Marina Warner (New York: Persea Books, 1982), I.1.1., pp. 3–4.
5. Ibid., I.1.1–2, p. 5.

The result was a literary explosion consisting of works by both men and women, in Latin and in vernacular languages: works enumerating the achievements of notable women; works rebutting the main accusations made against women; works arguing for the equal education of men and women; works defining and redefining women's proper role in the family, at court, and in public; and describing women's lives and experiences. Recent monographs and articles have begun to hint at the great range of this phenomenon, involving probably several thousand titles. The protofeminism of these "other voices" constitute a significant fraction of the literary product of the early modern era.

THE CATALOGUES Around 1365, the same Boccaccio whose *Corbaccio* rehearses the usual charges against female nature, wrote another work, *Concerning Famous Women*. A humanist treatise drawing on classical texts, it praised 106 notable women—one hundred of them from pagan Greek and Roman antiquity, and six from the religious and cultural tradition since antiquity—and helped make all readers aware of a sex normally condemned or forgotten. Boccaccio's outlook, nevertheless, is misogynist, for it singled out for praise those women who possessed the traditional virtues of chastity, silence, and obedience. Women who were active in the public realm, for example, rulers and warriors, were depicted as suffering terrible punishments for entering into the masculine sphere. Women were his subject, but Boccaccio's standard remained male.

Christine de Pizan's *Book of the City of Ladies* contains a second catalogue, one responding specifically to Boccaccio's. Where Boccaccio portrays female virtue as exceptional, she depicts it as universal. Many women in history were leaders, or remained chaste despite the lascivious approaches of men, or were visionaries and brave martyrs.

The work of Boccaccio inspired a series of catalogues of illustrious women of the biblical, classical, Christian, and local past: works by Alvaro de Luna, Jacopo Filippo Foresti (1497), Brantôme, Pierre Le Moyne, Pietro Paolo de Ribera (who listed 845 figures), and many others. Whatever their embedded prejudices, these catalogues of illustrious women drove home to the public the possibility of female excellence.

THE DEBATE At the same time, many questions remained: Could a woman be virtuous? Could she perform noteworthy deeds? Was she even, strictly speaking, of the same human species as men? These questions were debated over four centuries, in French, German, Italian, Spanish and English, by authors male and female, among Catholics, Protestants and Jews, in ponderous volumes and breezy pamphlets. The whole literary phenomenon has been called the *querelle des femmes*, the "Woman Question."

The opening volley of this battle occurred in the first years of the fifteenth century, in a literary debate sparked by Christine de Pizan. She ex-
changed letters critical of Jean de Meun's contribution to the *Romance of the
Rose* with two French humanists and royal secretaries, Jean de Montreuil and
Gontier Col. When the matter became public, Jean Gerson, one of Europe's
leading theologians, supported de Pizan's arguments against de Meun, for
the moment silencing the opposition.

The debate resurfaced repeatedly over the next two hundred years. *The
Triumph of Women* (1438) by Juan Rodríguez de la Camara (or Juan Rodríguez
del Padron) struck a new note by presenting arguments for the superiority
of women to men. *The Champion of Women* (1440–42) by Martin Le Franc
addresses once again the misogynist claims of *The Romance of the Rose*, and
offers counterevidence of female virtue and achievement.

A cameo of the debate on women is included in the *Courtier*, one of the
most-read books of the era, published by the Italian Baldassare Castiglione
in 1528 and immediately translated into other European vernaculars. The
Courtier depicts a series of evenings at the court of the Duke of Urbino in
which many men and some women of the highest social stratum amuse
themselves by discussing a range of literary and social issues. The "woman
question" is a pervasive theme throughout, and the third of its four books is
devoted entirely to that issue.

In a verbal duel, Gasparo Pallavicino and Giuliano de' Medici present
the main claims of the two traditions—the prevailing misogynist one, and
the newly emerging alternative one. Gasparo argues the innate inferiority
of women and their inclination to vice. Only in bearing children do they
profit the world. Giuliano counters that women share the same spiritual and
mental capacities as men and may excel in wisdom and action. Men and
women are of the same essence: just as no stone can be more perfectly a
stone than another, so no human being can be more perfectly human than
others, whether male or female. It was an astonishing assertion, boldly made
to an audience as large as all Europe.

THE TREATISES Humanism provided the materials for a positive count-
erconcept to the misogyny embedded in scholastic philosophy and law, and
inherited from the Greek, Roman and Christian pasts. A series of humanist
treatises on marriage and family, education and deportment, and on the
nature of women helped construct these new perspectives.

The works by Francesco Barbaro and Leon Battista Alberti, respectively
On Marriage (1415) and *On the Family* (1434–37), far from defending female
equality, reasserted women's responsibilities for rearing children and manag-
ing the housekeeping while being obedient, chaste, and silent. Neverthe-

less, they served the cause of reexamining the issue of women's nature by placing domestic issues at the center of scholarly concern and reopening the pertinent classical texts. In addition, Barbaro emphasized the companionate nature of marriage and the importance of a wife's spiritual and mental qualities for the well-being of the family.

These themes reappear in later humanist works on marriage and the education of women by Juan Luis Vives and Erasmus. Both were moderately sympathetic to the condition of women, without reaching beyond the usual masculine prescriptions for female behavior.

An outlook more favorable to women characterizes the nearly unknown work *In Praise of Women* (ca. 1487) by the Italian humanist Bartolomeo Goggio. In addition to providing a catalogue of illustrious women, Goggio argued that male and female are the same in essence, but that women (reworking from quite a new angle the Adam and Eve narrative) are actually superior. In the same vein, the Italian humanist Mario Equicola asserted the spiritual equality of men and women in *On Women* (1501). In 1525, Galeazzo Flavio Capra (or Capella) published his work *On the Excellence and Dignity of Women*. This humanist tradition of treatises defending the worthiness of women culminates in the work of Henricus Cornelius Agrippa *On the Nobility and Preeminence of the Female Sex*. No work by a male humanist more succinctly or explicitly presents the case for female dignity.

THE WITCH BOOKS While humanists grappled with the issues pertaining to women and family, other learned men turned their attention to what they perceived as a very great problem: witches. Witch-hunting manuals, explorations of the witch phenomenon, and even defenses of witches are not at first glance pertinent to the tradition of the other voice. But they do relate in this way: most accused witches were women. The hostility aroused by supposed witch activity is comparable to the hostility aroused by women. The evil deeds the victims of the hunt were charged with were exaggerations of the vices to which, many believed, all women were prone.

The connection between the witch accusation and the hatred of women is explicit in the notorious witch-hunting manual, *The Hammer of Witches* (1486), by two Dominican inquisitors, Heinrich Krämer and Jacob Sprenger. Here the inconstancy, deceitfulness, and lustfulness traditionally associated with women are depicted in exaggerated form as the core features of witch behavior. These inclined women to make a bargain with the devil—sealed by sexual intercourse—by which they acquired unholy powers. Such bizarre claims, far from being rejected by rational men, were broadcast by intellectuals. The German Ulrich Molitur, the Frenchman Nicolas Rémy, the Italian Stefano Guazzo coolly informed the public of sinister orgies and midnight pacts with the devil. The celebrated French jurist, historian, and political philosopher Jean Bodin argued that, because women were especially prone to diabolism, regular legal procedures could properly be suspended in order to try those accused of this "exceptional crime."

A few experts, such as the physician Johann Weyer, a student of Agrippa's, raised their voices in protest. In 1563, he explained the witch phenomenon thus, without discarding belief in diabolism: the devil deluded foolish old women afflicted by melancholia, causing them to believe that they had magical powers. Weyer's rational skepticism, which had good credibility in the community of the learned, worked to revise the conventional views of women and witchcraft.

WOMEN'S WORKS To the many categories of works produced on the question of women's worth must be added nearly all works written by women. A woman writing was in herself a statement of women's claim to dignity.

Only a few women wrote anything prior to the dawn of the modern era, for three reasons. First, they rarely received the education that would enable them to write. Second, they were not admitted to the public roles— as administrator, bureaucrat, lawyer or notary, university professor—in which they might gain knowledge of the kinds of things the literate public thought worth writing about. Third, the culture imposed silence upon women, considering speaking out a form of unchastity. Given these conditions, it is remarkable that any women wrote. Those who did before the fourteenth century were almost always nuns or religious women whose isolation made their pronouncements more acceptable.

From the fourteenth century on, the volume of women's writings crescendoed. Women continued to write devotional literature, although not always as cloistered nuns. They also wrote diaries, often intended as keepsakes for their children; books of advice to their sons and daughters; letters to family members and friends; and family memoirs, in a few cases elaborate enough to be considered histories.

A few women wrote works directly concerning the "woman question," and some of these, such as the humanists Isotta Nogarola, Cassandra Fedele, Laura Cereta, and Olimpia Morata, were highly trained. A few were professional writers, living by the income of their pen: the very first among them Christine de Pizan, noteworthy in this context as in so many others. In addition to *The Book of the City of Ladies* and her critiques of *The Romance of the Rose*, she wrote *The Treasure of the City of Ladies* (a guide to social decorum for women), an advice book for her son, much courtly verse, and a full-scale history of the reign of king Charles V of France.

WOMEN PATRONS Women who did not themselves write but encouraged others to do so boosted the development of an alternative tradition. Highly placed women patrons supported authors, artists, musicians, poets, and learned men. Such patrons, drawn mostly from the Italian elites and the courts of northern Europe, figure disproportionately as the dedicatees of the important works of early feminism.

For a start, it might be noted that the catalogues of Boccaccio and Alvaro de Luna were dedicated to the Florentine noblewoman Andrea Acciaiuoli and to Doña María, first wife of King Juan II of Castile, while the French translation of Boccaccio's work was commissioned by Anne of Brittany, wife of King Charles VIII of France. The humanist treatises of Goggio, Equicola, Vives, and Agrippa were dedicated, respectively, to Eleanora of Aragon, wife of Ercole I d'Este, duke of Ferrara; to Margherita Cantelma of Mantua; to Catherine of Aragon, wife of King Henry VIII of England; and to Margaret, duchess of Austria and regent of the Netherlands. As late as 1696, Mary Astell's *Serious Proposal to the Ladies, for the Advancement of Their True and Greatest Interest* was dedicated to Princess Ann of Denmark.

These authors presumed that their efforts would be welcome to female patrons, or they may have written at the bidding of those patrons. Silent themselves, perhaps even unresponsive, these loftily placed women helped shape the tradition of the other voice.

THE ISSUES The literary forms and patterns in which the tradition of the other voice presented itself have now been sketched. It remains to highlight the major issues about which this tradition crystallizes. In brief, there are four problems to which our authors return again and again, in plays and catalogues, in verse and in letters, in treatises and dialogues, in every language: the problem of chastity; the problem of power; the problem of speech; and the problem of knowledge. Of these the greatest, preconditioning the others, is the problem of chastity.

THE PROBLEM OF CHASTITY In traditional European culture, as in those of antiquity and others around the globe, chastity was perceived as woman's quintessential virtue—in contrast to courage, or generosity, or leadership, or rationality, seen as virtues characteristic of men. Opponents of women charged them with insatiable lust. Women themselves and their defenders—without disputing the validity of the standard—responded that women were capable of chastity.

The requirement of chastity kept women at home, silenced them, isolated them, left them in ignorance. It was the source of all other impediments. Why was it so important to the society of men, of whom chastity was not required, and who, more often than not, considered it their right to violate the chastity of any woman they encountered?

Female chastity ensured the continuity of the male-headed household.

If a man's wife was not chaste, he could not be sure of the legitimacy of his offspring. If they were not his, and they acquired his property, it was not his household, but some other man's, that had endured. If his daughter was not chaste, she could not be transferred to another man's household as his wife, and he was dishonored.

The whole system of the integrity of the household and the transmission of property was bound up in female chastity. Such a requirement only pertained to property-owning classes, of course. Poor women could not expect to maintain their chastity, least of all if they were in contact with high-status men to whom all women but those of their own household were prey.

In Catholic Europe, the requirement of chastity was further buttressed by moral and religious imperatives. Original sin was inextricably linked with the sexual act. Virginity was seen as heroic virtue, far more impressive than, say, the avoidance of idleness or greed. Monasticism, the cultural institution that dominated medieval Europe for centuries, was grounded in the renunciation of the flesh. The Catholic reform of the eleventh century imposed a similar standard on all the clergy, and a heightened awareness of sexual requirements on all the laity. Although men were asked to be chaste, female unchastity was much worse: it led to the devil, as Eve had led mankind to sin.

To such requirements, women and their defenders protested their innocence. More, following the example of holy women who had escaped the requirements of family and sought the religious life, some women began to conceive of female communities as alternatives both to family and to the cloister. Christine de Pizan's city of ladies was such a community. Moderata Fonte and Mary Astell envisioned others. The luxurious salons of the French *précieuses* of the seventeenth century, or the comfortable English drawing rooms of the next, may have been born of the same impulse. Here women might not only escape, if briefly, the subordinate position that life in the family entailed, but they might make claims to power, exercise their capacity for speech, and display their knowledge.

THE PROBLEM OF POWER Women were excluded from power: the whole cultural tradition insisted upon it. Only men were citizens, only men bore arms, only men could be chiefs or lords or kings. There were exceptions which did not disprove the rule, when wives or widows or mothers took the place of men, awaiting their return or the maturation of a male heir. A woman who attempted to rule in her own right was perceived as an anomaly, a monster, at once a deformed woman and an insufficient male, sexually confused and, consequently, unsafe.

The association of such images with women who held or sought power explains some otherwise odd features of early modern culture. Queen Elizabeth I of England, one of the few women to hold full regal authority in European history, played with such male/female images—positive ones, of course—in representing herself to her subjects. She was a prince, and manly, even though she was female. She was also (she claimed) virginal, a condition absolutely essential if she was to avoid the attacks of her opponents. Catherine de' Medici, who ruled France as widow and regent for her sons, also adopted such imagery in defining her position. She chose as one symbol the figure of Artemisia, an androgynous ancient warrior-heroine, who combined a female persona with masculine powers.

Power in a woman, without such sexual imagery, seems to have been indigestible by the culture. A rare note was struck by the Englishman Sir Thomas Elyot in his *Defence of Good Women* (1540), justifying both women's participation in civic life and prowess in arms. The old tune was sung by the Scots reformer John Knox in his *First Blast of the Trumpet against the Monstrous Regiment of Women* (1558), for whom rule by women, defective in nature, was a hideous contradiction in terms.

The confused sexuality of the imagery of female potency was not reserved for rulers. Any woman who excelled was likely to be called an Amazon, recalling the self-mutilated warrior women of antiquity who repudiated all men, gave up their sons, and raised only their daughters. She was often said to have "exceeded her sex," or to have possessed "masculine virtue"—as the very fact of conspicuous excellence conferred masculinity, even on the female subject. The catalogues of notable women often showed those female heroes dressed in armor, armed to the teeth, like men. Amazonian heroines romp through the epics of the age—Ariosto's *Orlando Furioso* (1532), Spenser's *Faerie Queene* (1590–1609). Excellence in a woman was perceived as a claim for power, and power was reserved for the masculine realm. A woman who possessed either was masculinized, and lost title to her own female identity.

THE PROBLEM OF SPEECH Just as power had a sexual dimension when it was claimed by women, so did speech. A good woman spoke little. Excessive speech was an indication of unchastity. By speech, women seduced men. Eve had lured Adam into sin by her speech. Accused witches were commonly accused of having spoken abusively, or irrationally, or simply too much. As enlightened a figure as Francesco Barbaro insisted on silence in a woman, which he linked to her perfect unanimity with her husband's will and her unblemished virtue (her chastity). Another Italian humanist, Leonardo Bruni, in advising a noblewoman on her studies, barred her not from speech, but from public speaking. That was reserved for men.

Related to the problem of speech was that of costume, another, if silent, form of self-expression. Assigned the task of pleasing men as their primary occupation, elite women often tended to elaborate costume, hairdressing, and the use of cosmetics. Clergy and secular moralists alike condemned these practices. The appropriate function of costume and adornment was to announce the status of a woman's husband or father. Any further indulgence in adornment was akin to unchastity.

THE PROBLEM OF KNOWLEDGE When the Italian noblewoman Isotta Nogarola had begun to attain a reputation as a humanist, she was accused of incest—a telling instance of the association of learning in women with unchastity. That chilling association inclined any woman who was educated to deny that she was, or to make exaggerated claims of heroic chastity.

If educated women were pursued with suspicions of sexual misconduct, women seeking an education faced an even more daunting obstacle: the assumption that women were by nature incapable of learning, that reason was a particularly masculine ability. Just as they proclaimed their chastity, women and their defenders insisted upon their capacity for learning. The major work by a male writer on female education—*On the Education of a Christian Woman*, by Juan Luis Vives (1523)—granted female capacity for intellection, but argued still that a woman's whole education was to be shaped around the requirement of chastity and a future within the household. Female writers of the next generations—Marie de Gournay in France, Anna Maria van Schurman in Holland, Mary Astell in England—began to envision other possibilities.

The pioneers of female education were the Italian women humanists who managed to attain a Latin literacy and knowledge of classical and Christian literature equivalent to that of prominent men. Their works implicitly and explicitly raise questions about women's social roles, defining problems that beset women attempting to break out of the cultural limits that had bound them. Like Christine de Pizan, who achieved an advanced education through her father's tutoring and her own devices, their bold questioning makes clear the importance of training. Only when women were educated to the same standard as male leaders would they be able to raise that other voice and insist on their dignity as human beings morally, intellectually, and legally equal to men.

THE OTHER VOICE The other voice, a voice of protest, was mostly female, but also male. It spoke in the vernaculars and in Latin, in treatises and dialogues, plays and poetry, letters and diaries and pamphlets. It battered at the wall of misogynist beliefs that encircled women and raised a banner announcing its claims. The female was equal (or even superior) to the male in essential nature—moral, spiritual, intellectual. Women were capable of higher education, of holding positions of power and influence in the public realm, and of speaking and writing persuasively. The last bastion of masculine supremacy, centered on the notions of a woman's primary domestic responsibility and the requirement of female chastity, was not as yet assaulted—although visions of productive female communities as alternatives to the family indicated an awareness of the problem.

During the period 1300 to 1700, the other voice remained only a voice, and one only dimly heard. It did not result—yet—in an alteration of social patterns. Indeed, to this day, they have not entirely been altered. Yet the call for justice issued as long as six centuries ago by those writing in the tradition of the other voice must be recognized as the source and origin of the mature feminist tradition and of the realignment of social institutions accomplished in the modern age.

We would like to thank the volume editors in this series, who responded with many suggestions to an earlier draft of this introduction, making it a collaborative enterprise. Many of their suggestions and criticisms have resulted in revisions of this introduction, though we remain responsible for the final product.

PROJECTED TITLES IN THE SERIES

Giuseppa Eleonora Barbapiccola and Diamante Medaglia Faini, *The Education of Women*, edited and translated by Paula Findlen and Rebecca Messbarger

Marie Dentière, *Prefaces, Epistles, and History of the Deliverance of Geneva by the Protestants*, edited and translated by Mary B. McKinley

Isabella d'Este, *Selected Letters*, edited and translated by Deanna Shemek

Marie de Gournay, *The Equality of Men and Women and Other Writings*, edited and translated by Richard Hillman and Colette Quesnel

Annibale Guasco, *Discussion with D. Lavinia, His Daughter, concerning the Manner of Conducting Oneself at Court*, edited and translated by Peggy Osborn

Olympia Morata, *Complete Writings*, edited and translated by Holt N. Parker

Isotta Nogarola, *Selected Letters*, edited by Margaret King and Albert Rabil Jr. and translated by Diana Robin, with an introduction by Margaret L. King

Christine de Pizan, *Debate over the "Romance of the Rose,"* edited and translated by Tom Conley

François Poulain de la Barre, *The Equality of the Sexes and the Education of Women*, edited and translated by Albert Rabil Jr.

Olivia Sabuco, *The New Philosophy: True Medicine*, edited and translated by Gianna Pomata

ABBREVIATIONS

r (Latin *recto*)   Front side of a manuscript leaf (righthand page in a bound volume)

v (Latin *verso*)   Back side of a manuscript leaf (lefthand page in a bound volume)

VaAS   Vatican City, Archivio Segreto Vaticano

VeAP   Venice, Archivio Storico del Patriarcato di Venezia

VeAS   Venice, Archivio di Stato

NUOVA PIANTA
DELL'
INCLITA CITTA'
DI VENEZIA
Regolata l'Anno 17...
...la di Piero, e Venti...

Canal della

Lodovico Ughi, *Nuova Pianta della Inclita Città di Venetia regolata l'anno 1799* (Venice: Ludovico Furlanetto, 1797; originally produced in 1729). 67 × 63 cm. Chicago, Newberry Library, Novacco Map Collection, 6F 32. (Photograph: Newberry Library)

AUTOBIOGRAPHY

OF AN

ASPIRING SAINT

Last leaf of Cecilia Ferrazzi's autobiography. Venice, Archivio di Stato, Sant'Ufficio, busta 112, "Contra Ceciliam Ferrazzi de affectata sanctitate," fol. 86r. Ferrazzi's signature is in the middle of the page. The top half of the page was written by her amanuensis, Friar Antonio da Venezia; the bottom half by Andrea Vescovi, chancellor of the Venetian Inquisition. (Photograph: Venice, Archivio di Stato)

INTRODUCTION

THE OTHER VOICE

More and more scholars of early modern Europe are seeking to locate and listen to women's voices—voices that spoke briefly to their contemporaries but then, through suppression or neglect, fell silent. These voices come almost exclusively from the upper social strata. Given a motive, an opportunity, and a certain amount of courage, a woman whose family's rank and resources enabled her to acquire an education could take pen in hand to address one or more readers in her own generation, and potentially an audience in the distant future. Lacking these privileges and opportunities, the vast majority of women—though their activities left traces in many types of records, from tax rolls to parish registers—did not, because they could not, articulate their opinions, aspirations, and dreams in any form that permits us to hear their voices.

Social historians have shown, however, that there *are* ways of "listening to the inarticulate." Perhaps the best is to examine the records of judicial proceedings, particularly Inquisition trials. In tribunals of the Roman Inquisition, the words of plaintiffs, defendants, and witnesses (from the late sixteenth century on, a considerable proportion of them female) were not summarized or reported in indirect discourse, as was the practice in many other courts, but taken down verbatim.[1] So were the questions posed by the in-

1. Roman and Anglo-American law differ so much that the English terms *plaintiff, suspect, accused*, and *defendant* can convey only approximately the precise status of a person before the court at any given moment. For a lucid outline of Inquisition procedure, see John Tedeschi, "Organization and Procedures of the Roman Inquisition: A Sketch," in *The Prosecution of Heresy: Collected Studies on the Inquisition in Early Modern Italy* (Binghamton, N.Y.: Medieval and Renaissance Texts and Studies, 1991), pp. 132–53. In the first four decades of its existence the Roman Inquisition tried very few women. Beginning in the 1580s, when sorcery replaced philo-Protestantism as the offense most often prosecuted, the gender balance shifted dramatically. See Anne Jacobson Schutte, "I processi dell'Inquisizione veneziana nel Seicento: La femminilizzazione dell'eresia,"

quisitors. Hence the transcript of an Inquisition trial records a conversation or dialogue, in which we can hear one voice responding to another.

What kind of dialogue? Certainly not a spontaneous conversation between equals. To be sure, when summoned before an Inquisition tribunal for interrogation, practically all suspects talked, sometimes at considerable length, about their life experiences—but their accounts were shaped by the inquisitor's agenda. He asked the questions, beginning sometimes with open-ended ones (as in Ferrazzi's case) but moving eventually to demands for more specific information. The suspect had to furnish answers, the truthfulness of which the inquisitor and his colleagues evaluated in terms of what they considered plausible and likely and in comparison to what witnesses had said.

Given that the inquisitor directed the dialogue, how clearly and directly do the voices of defendants and witnesses come through to us? All too many scholars, evading the question or not even recognizing that an epistemological problem exists, treat trial transcripts as if they were tape recordings of voices spontaneously recounting exactly what they had done and believed.[2] Two Italian historians who confront the problem directly come to opposite conclusions. Carlo Ginzburg is relatively optimistic about the possibility of capturing the authentic voices of suspects, defendants, and witnesses by making use of an intellectual tool he calls a filter. When persons being interrogated merely parrot what they know or guess the inquisitor wants to hear, all that passes through the filter is his voice in distorted form; but when they articulate ideas that take the inquisitor by surprise, then we can be confident that we are actually hearing them speak.[3] According to Andrea Del Col, on the contrary, we must keep firmly in mind that employees of the Holy Office made trial transcripts for the court's own purposes: to discover and punish heresy. In no sense, therefore, can court

in *L'Inquisizione romana in Italia nell'età moderna: Archivi, problemi di metodo e nuove ricerche,* ed. Andrea Del Col and Giovanna Paolin (Rome: Ministero per i Beni Culturali e Ambientali, Ufficio Centrale per i Beni Archivistici, 1991), pp. 159–73.

2. For an ingenious but not entirely successful attempt to recover women's voices from proceedings of German secular courts, in which defendants' and witnesses' testimony was summarized in indirect discourse, see Lyndal Roper, *Oedipus and the Devil: Witchcraft, Sexuality, and Religion in Early Modern Europe* (London: Routledge, 1994).

3. Carlo Ginzburg, *The Cheese and the Worms: The Cosmos of a Sixteenth-Century Miller,* trans. John Tedeschi and Anne C. Tedeschi (Baltimore: Johns Hopkins University Press, 1980; rpt., Harmondsworth, Middlesex, England: Penguin, 1982). In a subsequent publication, he suggests (none too plausibly) that inquisitors sought in a proto-scientific way to explore the beliefs of the people whom they put on trial: Carlo Ginzburg, "The Inquisitor as Anthropologist," in *Clues, Myths, and the Historical Method,* trans. John Tedeschi and Anne C. Tedeschi (Baltimore: Johns Hopkins University Press, 1989), pp. 156–64.

records be considered "primary sources" for the lives and ideas of the people being interrogated.[4]

The texts in this volume enable us both to test these hypotheses and to avoid some of the problems they identify. Among the many thousands of records of Inquisition investigations and prosecutions preserved in Italian archives, the massive transcript of Cecilia Ferrazzi's trial by the Venetian Holy Office in 1664–65, a small portion of which appears in translation here,[5] presents an exceptional feature. At the end of her fourth appearance in court for interrogation, Ferrazzi audaciously requested and was granted the chance to tell her story in her own way—that is, to present a continuous narrative shaped by herself, as opposed to furnishing isolated fragments of her life experience in response to the inquisitor's questions. Thus her voice reaches us not only as testimony furnished on demand but also in an alternative, most unusual form: an inquisitorial autobiography.[6]

Since readers of this volume will encounter Ferrazzi's story twice, first as elicited by the inquisitor and then as she chose to recount it, retelling it here would be superfluous. A more pressing task is to set her autobiography in context by exploring the circumstances in which she produced it. Had she not been put on trial by the Inquisition, Ferrazzi would never have committed the "autobiographical act"[7] in a form accessible to us. First on our agenda, therefore, is an introduction to the Roman Inquisition and its operation in Venice. Then we shall examine several issues essential to an under-

---

4. Andrea Del Col, "I processi dell'Inquisizione come fonte: Considerazioni diplomatiche e storiche," *Annuario dell'Istituto Storico Italiano per l'Età Moderna e Contemporanea* 35–36 (1983–84): 31–49; Del Col, "Alcune osservazioni sui processi inquisitoriali come fonti storiche," *Metodi e ricerche: Rivista di studi regionali*, n. s. 13 (1994): 85–105. See also his edition of the trials studied by Ginzburg in *The Cheese and the Worms*: Andrea Del Col, ed., *Domenico Scandella detto Menocchio: I processi dell'Inquisizione (1583–1599)* (Pordenone: Biblioteca dell'Immagine, 1990); English version, *Domenico Scandella Known as Menocchio: His Trials before the Inquisition (1583–1599)*, trans. John Tedeschi and Anne C. Tedeschi (Binghamton, N.Y.: Medieval and Renaissance Texts and Studies, 1996).

5. VeAS, Sant'Ufficio, busta 112 (cited hereafter as Trial Record), "Contra Ceciliam Ferrazzi de affectata sanctitate" (Against Cecilia Ferrazzi for Pretense of Sanctity). The portion presented here—the first four interrogations of Ferrazzi and her autobiography—was issued previously as Cecilia Ferrazzi, *Autobiografia di una santa mancata*, ed. Anne Jacobson Schutte (Bergamo: Pierluigi Lubrina, 1990).

6. I know of no other autobiography self-generated during a trial conducted by the Roman Inquisition. On a Spanish inquisitorial autobiography, see Adrienne Schizzano Mandel, "Le procès inquisitorial comme acte autobiographique: Le cas de Sor María de San Jerónimo," in *L'autobiographie dans le monde hispanique* (Aix-en-Provence: Université de Provence, 1980), pp. 155–69.

7. I have borrowed this felicitous term from Elizabeth W. Bruss, *Autobiographical Acts: The Changing Situation of a Literary Genre* (Baltimore: Johns Hopkins University Press, 1976).

standing of Ferrazzi's life-writing: purity and danger, writing and speaking, power and obedience, and pretense.

THE ROMAN INQUISITION AND VENICE

In many people's minds, the word *Inquisition* conjures up a horde of specters: dank rooms stocked with instruments of torture, mercilessly employed; public burnings of victims at the stake; carefully coordinated campaigns conducted by the Church, with the government's blessing, against individual "deviants" (Protestants, witches) and entire minority groups ("New Christians" of Jewish and Muslim origin); or, conversely, thought control exercised by an obscurantist Church in perennial conflict with that wave of the future, the enlightened secular state. Before we go any further, these ghosts must be laid to rest.

In the first place, the "black legend" of the Inquisition constructed by historians from the eighteenth to the early twentieth century is a myth. Recent scholarship has demonstrated that, as John Tedeschi puts it, an Inquisition tribunal was not "a drumhead court, a chamber of horrors, or a judicial labyrinth from which escape was impossible."[8] In fact, Inquisition courts offered by far the best criminal justice available in early modern Europe. Procedural rules mandated by central directorates, spelled out in manuals, and rigorously enforced through close supervision of functionaries in the field required the keeping of verbatim transcripts, provided counsel for those accused, and allowed them to mount a defense. These regulations, furthermore, placed strict limitations on the acceptance of hearsay evidence, the application of torture, and the execution of convicted heretics.[9] Ferrazzi, for instance, was never tortured, and she ran no risk of being put to death. Therefore, although no responsible person in the late twentieth century would endorse the objectives of the Holy Office, we know enough about its operations to refrain from equating them with those of modern totalitarian dictatorships.

Though modeled on the inquisitions in the Spanish kingdoms, the Roman Inquisition, unlike its Iberian counterparts, was not a department of a secular state. Early in the thirteenth century the Church had established a

8. Tedeschi, *The Prosecution of Heresy*, p. 8.

9. Ibid., passim; John Tedeschi, "The Status of the Defendant before the Roman Inquisition," in *Ketzerverfolgung im 16. und frühen 17. Jahrhundert*, ed. Hans Rudolf Guggisberg, Bernd Moeller, and Silvana Seidel Menchi, Wolfenbütteler Forschungen 51 (Wiesbaden: Harrassowitz, 1992), pp. 125–46.

network of inquisitorial courts to deal with what it considered the most prevalent and dangerous heresy of that era, Catharist dualism. In 1542 Pope Paul III radically transformed and rejuvenated the system to confront the Protestant challenge. The new Roman Inquisition was governed by the Congregation of the Holy Office, a committee of cardinals over which the pope presided. Observant Dominican and Conventual Franciscan inquisitors named by the Congregation headed provincial tribunals. The Roman Inquisition operated only on the Italian peninsula (not including Sicily), in the papal territory around Avignon in southern France, and on the island of Malta. Elsewhere in Catholic Europe outside Iberia, bishops prosecuted heresy as they had under the old system.[10]

For the Roman Inquisition to function in Italian polities other than the States of the Church, Paul III and his successors needed initial acceptance by and subsequent cooperation from secular governments, both of which they obtained. Those who ran early modern states, along with the overwhelming majority of their subjects, were only occasionally and superficially Machiavellian secularists. The sharp conceptual and operational distinctions we make today between sacred and secular, church and state were not part of their mental furniture. Princes and civil servants shared with prelates and priests several fundamental assumptions: that Christian truth was one and indivisible; that it must be manifested on earth by a single church; and that all those in authority, as well as their subjects, must cooperate in conforming to the will of God and promoting his purposes.

Venice is no exception to this rule. Contrary to an older view that the Most Serene Republic was a harbinger of modern secularism in continual, irrepressible conflict with the Papacy, recent scholarship has made clear that the men who ran the Republic and those in charge of the Church agreed about the ultimate purposes of a Christian society.[11] On the means for achieving these ends, however, consensus was by no means easy to reach. Venice and Rome frequently collided on jurisdictional issues, such as whether all bishops appointed to serve in Venetian territory should be Venetian subjects, under what circumstances (if any) defendants on trial in ecclesiastical courts in the Republic could be extradited to papal territory,[12] and how to regulate the conveyance and taxation of property. Although

10. Recent specialized scholarship is well represented in Del Col and Paolin, eds., *L'Inquisizione romana in Italia nell'età moderna.*

11. For a review of modern scholarship on Venice, see James S. Grubb, "When Myths Lose Power: Four Decades of Venetian Historiography," *Journal of Modern History* 58 (1986): 43–94.

12. On extradition, see Carlo De Frede, "L'estradizione degli eretici dal Dominio veneziano nel Cinquecento," *Atti dell'Accademia Pontiana,* n. s. 20 (1970–71): 255–86.

these disputes escalated into a major confrontation only once, in the Interdict Crisis of 1605–7, diplomatic dispatches and other documentary sources reveal constant tension in the relationship between Venice and the Holy See.

Chief among the matters giving rise to such tension was the prosecution of heresy. As Tedeschi and William Monter put it, "any branch of the Roman Inquisition located in the domains of an aggressive secular ruler labored under some set of special disabilities."[13] Del Col has fleshed out this accurate generalization for the early years in which the Roman Inquisition operated in Venice. He has shown how adroitly the Venetians maneuvered during the 1540s and 1550s to secure a governmental presence in inquisitorial proceedings more significant than any other state managed to attain. Through the regular participation in all trials of lay representatives, the Republic strove to protect its subjects against arbitrary actions by overzealous or unscrupulous inquisitors and to shield them from extradition. In Venice, these lay representatives were the Tre Savi all'Eresia (three wise men on heresy), elected by the Senate from among its most experienced and distinguished members; in subject cities, the representative was the rector or his designate. The rulers of Venice did not cede to the Inquisition all responsibility for ferreting out manifestations of unorthodoxy. Through correspondence with rectors and ambassadors, key government bodies (notably the Council of Ten) kept an eye on individuals and groups engaged in what appeared to be superstitious, scandalous, or unorthodox activities.[14]

As suggested earlier, inquisitors took sole charge of questioning. Other members of the tribunal included the papal nuncio or his auditor, the patriarch of Venice or his vicar general, and one or more of the Tre Savi. Support personnel were also regularly present, including the procurator fiscal and the chancellor, who were appointed by and responsible to the inquisitor. In Venetian trial transcripts, these other officials almost never open their mouths. To infer that the inquisitor's colleagues were mere silent presences in the courtroom, however, would be a mistake. It seems certain that when defendants and witnesses were not present, representatives of the Venetian church and state had their say. Procedural decisions, which were summarized rather than recorded in direct discourse, were made collegially.

13. John Tedeschi with William Monter, "Toward a Statistical Profile of the Italian Inquisitions, Sixteenth to Eighteenth Centuries," in Tedeschi, *The Prosecution of Heresy*, p. 91.

14. Andrea Del Col, "Organizzazione, composizione e giurisdizione dei tribunali dell'Inquisizione romana nella repubblica di Venezia (1500–1550)," *Critica storica* 25 (1988): 244–94; Del Col, "L'Inquisizione romana e il potere politico nella repubblica di Venezia (1540–1560)," *Critica storica* 28 (1991): 189–250. On the lay deputies, see also Paul F. Grendler, "The 'Tre Savii sopra Eresia,' 1547–1605: A Prosopographical Study," *Studi veneziani*, n. s. 3 (1979): 283–340.

Since representatives of the secular government attended sessions in the chapel of San Teodoro, where the Holy Office met,[15] what went on there was no secret to the highest officials of the government. If they chose, they could work through official diplomatic channels or use informal means to apply pressure in Rome on behalf of a defendant. As we shall see, the final outcome of Ferrazzi's case was decisively influenced in this way.

PURITY AND DANGER

Like all Catholic girls in the artisan, professional, and aristocratic classes during this era, Cecilia Ferrazzi, born in Venice in 1609,[16] grew up knowing that eventually she would either marry or become a nun. For her, the choice was clear: she must preserve her virginity—her "purity," as she usually said—by dedicating it to Christ. Her father, an artisan who employed several assistants, was prosperous enough to support a large family and to contemplate furnishing a dowry for his only daughter. Initially he and her mother urged Cecilia to marry, but then, after the belated and unexpected birth of her sister Maria, they agreed to finance her entry into a convent instead. When their death in the plague epidemic of 1630 aborted this plan, Ferrazzi and those who took charge of her confronted the serious dilemma of how to safeguard her chastity.

To use the term current at the time, the orphaned twenty-year-old Ferrazzi was a *putta pericolante*, a "girl in danger," as she and everyone else realized. Her preoccupation with possible assaults on her purity, a central theme in her autobiography, should not be taken to mean that she was what we would call paranoid on this subject. In early modern Europe, unmarried girls and young women bereft of close supervision by respectable adults (preferably women) ran the grave risk of being seduced or sexually assaulted, after which they almost inevitably fell into prostitution. In a carefully chosen foster home, shelter, or convent, their purity and hence their prospects were presumably secure. For this reason Ferrazzi was placed *in*

15. See Anne Jacobson Schutte, "Uno spazio, tre poteri: San Teodoro, sede del Sant'Ufficio nella prima età moderna," In *San Marco: Aspetti storici ed agiografici*, ed. Antonio Niero (Venice: Marsilio, 1996), pp. 97–109.

16. She was baptized as Cecilia Corona in the church of San Lio on 20 April 1609; her father's profession was erroneously given as *marangon* (carpenter) instead of *casseler* (boxmaker) and her mother's name as Nadalina rather than Maddalena (VeAP, San Lio, Battesimi 1 [1566–1638]). These errors in the record of Cecilia's baptism and the birth eighteen months later of a sister named Corona, who died on 19 October 1614 (VeAP, San Lio, Battesimi 1; VeAP, Santa Marina, Morti 3), caused confusion during Cecilia's trial. She was accused of lying about her name as well as feigning holiness.

salvo (literally, "in safety") in the custody of people able and willing to protect her.

Around 1648 the opportunity to assist other "girls in danger" presented
itself to Ferrazzi. She began as governess of the patrician Paolo Lion's two
motherless daughters while he was away from Venice on government service. Soon she began to take under her wing other girls from various social
classes. Almost by chance, she had found her vocation. As the number of
her charges multiplied, she attracted wealthy supporters willing to under-
write the much-needed social service she was providing. Thus she was
able to move from her first house of refuge at San Lorenzo to increasingly
larger quarters at San Giovanni Evangelista, in Cannaregio, and finally at
Sant'Antonio di Castello. By the time of her arrest by the Inquisition in
June 1664, she was safeguarding, indoctrinating in piety, and training in
needlework about three hundred virgins ranging in age from five to just
under thirty.

How successfully did Ferrazzi protect her charges' purity? Questions
about her performance, which prompted the denunciation of Ferrazzi to
the Holy Office, pervade the trial record. Almost all patrician and clerical
witnesses praised her as the very model of a pious woman and lauded her
work as socially necessary and impeccably carried out. Many of her "girls,"
on the other hand, depicted her as proud and dictatorial, and complained
about poor living conditions and sadistic punishments in her houses. The
inquisitor, Agapito Ugoni, was interested primarily in other sorts of charges:
above all, that she had ventured beyond the role of surrogate mother by
hearing her charges' confessions and absolving them in a manner indistin-
guishable from sacramental confession.[17] In seventeenth-century eyes, preserving girls' virginity was a perfectly appropriate job for a woman; mediat-
ing their standing with God was a responsibility reserved to ordained men.

WRITING AND SPEAKING

The circumstances in which Ferrazzi was born and raised enabled her to
become literate. What exactly that means in her case is crucial to the understanding of her autobiography. Social historians gauge the extent of literacy
in any particular time and place, as well as its spread over generations or

---

17. Ferrazzi had adopted a disciplinary feature common in female and male religious orders:
the monthly "chapter of faults," in which novices and professed religious gathered before their
superiors to admit their shortcomings in public and receive admonition and punishment. Some
of her charges, as well as the inquisitor, however, chose tendentiously to interpret this practice
as sacramental confession.

centuries, in the only way the sources permit. Taking some type of document surviving in quantity that required parties to a transaction to authenticate it, they calculate the percentage of people who affixed their signatures, as opposed to those who made a mark (usually a cross). In Western Europe until the nineteenth century, basic education, whether acquired in school or in a less formal setting, was a two-stage process. First, learners mastered reading, at which point many of them stopped. A few, more males than females, entered the second stage: learning how to write. To specialists in literacy, therefore, it seems logical to assume that all those capable of signing their names could also read.

This method, though useful for estimating the degree of literacy in a large population, is unreliable for the study of individuals. Although the ability to write one's name indicates previous instruction in reading, it reveals nothing about a person's reading or writing habits. Fourteen times during the prosecution phase of Ferrazzi's lengthy trial, after the transcript of each interrogation was read back to her, she signed her name to acknowledge that her words had been recorded fully and accurately.[18] Yet not once during the fifteen-month trial did she or any of the hundreds of witnesses who testified against and for her refer in an unambiguous way to her reading.[19] Though Ferrazzi meets historians' formal criteria for literacy, she was clearly dependent upon the spoken word, both for acquiring information and for expressing herself. If the need arose to set down her words, she had to call on a hired pen, an amanuensis.

If we break the word *autobiography* into its component parts, Ferrazzi's account qualifies as a "self-life," but what about the third element, "-writing"? Friar Antonio da Venezia, the court-appointed scribe to whom she dictated her account, seems to deserve full credit for having produced the written work. But if we interpret *-graphy* as "composition," we can answer the question differently. Ferrazzi had extensive experience in oral composition of her life history. A difficult and intriguing penitent, she was required on numerous occasions by a succession of spiritual directors to make a general

18. Her awkward and vacillating signature indicates that she was not an experienced or skillful writer. For comparison, see Luisa Ciammitti, "One Saint Less: The Story of Angela Mellini, Bolognese Seamstress (1667–17[?])," in *Sex and Gender in Historical Perspective: Selections from "Quaderni Storici"*, ed. Edward Muir and Guido Ruggiero (Baltimore: Johns Hopkins University Press, 1990), pp. 141–76; and Armando Petrucci, "Note sulla scrittura di Angela Mellini," *Quaderni storici* 41 (May–August 1979): 640–43.

19. That she had her brothers read the lives of the saints and held an Office in her hand does not mean that she was actually reading. On a woman who probably could not read using a book as a devotional aid, see *The Book of Margery Kempe*, ed. and trans. B. A. Windeatt (Harmondsworth, Middlesex, England: Penguin, 1985), p. 56.

confession: to begin at the beginning of her life and recount it fully. By the time of her trial, therefore, she knew very well how to construct and present her story in a recognizable form.

Ferrazzi did not learn solely by doing. Hearing the lives of female saints read aloud at her mother's knee and many times thereafter provided a paradigm for composing an account of her own life. In addition, as an aspiring Carmelite nun whose younger sister managed to become one, she was no doubt very familiar with the self-produced life of a Carmelite saint, the spiritual autobiography of Teresa of Avila.[20] A proper holy woman's *vita*,[21] Ferrazzi was well aware, begins with the subject's birth and infancy and proceeds to a defining moment in her childhood or early adolescence, usually her decision to refuse marriage and espouse Christ. Then such a work turns topical: visions and miraculous experiences are recounted with little regard to the order in which they occurred.

If Ferrazzi had been able to enter a convent, a spiritual director might have ordered her to pick up a pen and try to record her life in what one scholar has called a "commanded autobiography," a general confession put on paper at the confessor's order.[22] More likely, given her rudimentary command of writing, he would have done the job himself. In either case, the result would have been a collaborative project—one in which the amount and quality of the subject's input is difficult if not impossible to determine. Censorship would have been imposed at every stage of composition: before writing and even before speaking, for the woman would have known in advance what the spiritual director expected and what he would reject as verging on heresy, and later, when he, his colleagues, and perhaps even the Holy Office would inspect the first draft and demand deletions and changes.[23]

20. Teresa's *Vida* first appeared in print in an edition of her works issued in Salamanca in 1588. An Italian translation by the Oratorian priest Giovanni Francesco Bordini, first published in Rome in 1599, was reissued many times thereafter. See Valentino Macca, O.C.D., "Presenza e influsso del magistero teresiano in Italia," in *Teresa de Jesús: Estudios histórico-literarios, Studi storico-letterari* (Rome: Teresianum, 1982), pp. 121–50.

21. The Latin term *vita* is used here for the life of a holy person, which is not a "biography" in the modern sense of the word. See Donald Weinstein and Rudolph Bell, *Saints and Society: The Two Worlds of Western Christendom, 1100–1700* (Chicago: University of Chicago Press, 1982), pp. 14–15.

22. Romeo De Maio, *Donna e Rinascimento* (Milan: Il Saggiatore, 1987), pp. 167–72.

23. For an astute assessment of one subject's input into her "commanded autobiography," see Alison Weber, *Teresa of Avila and the Rhetoric of Femininity* (Princeton: Princeton University Press, 1990). On the autobiographies of other Spanish nuns and beatas, see the recent study by Isabelle Poutrin, *Le voile et la plume: Autobiographie et sainteté dans l'Espagne moderne* (Madrid: Casa de Velásquez, 1995). More negative conclusions on this matter are reached by Jacques Le Brun, "Les biographies spirituelles françaises du XVIIème siècle: Écriture féminine? Écriture mys-

In the years immediately preceding her trial, Ferrazzi boasted that one of her Jesuit confessors was writing an account of her life.[24] If this *vita* was ever composed, it did not come to light during the trial or later. In its absence, Ferrazzi seized the opportunity of composing one herself with the help of an amanuensis whom she did not know, a scribe whose assignment gave him no opportunity to shape her account either before or after he set it down. But the dictated autobiography did not serve the purpose she had in mind, which was to rebut accusations already on the record. Instead, as the inquisitor's marks on the manuscript reveal, Ferrazzi's autobiography facilitated his task by highlighting issues to be pursued in the prosecution of its producer.

POWER AND OBEDIENCE

To a limited degree, as we have seen\ Ferrazzi was an acting subject who used the power of chastity to invent a vocation and the power of speech to construct a self-image set down in writing by Friar Antonio. In many other respects, she was an object under the power and control of others. Her choice of words bears out this observation. *Obedience* and *obey* occur fifty times in her autobiography, their contraries *disobedience* and *disobey* three times. Those whom she was required (and said she wanted) to obey she termed "superiors," a word she uses eight times.

Who were these superiors, and what did obedience to them entail? First in chronological order come her mother and father. She remembers them with affectionate respect even as she recalls the heavy responsibilities for housework and care of siblings placed on her by her mother and both parents' initial opposition to her becoming a nun. In the autobiography she presents herself as a dutiful daughter who sought anxiously to avoid even the most trivial forms of disobedience. She did not claim to have accomplished this feat alone. In early childhood she became used to supplicating Christ, the Virgin Mary, certain saints, and living holy people for assistance in being obedient to her human superiors. On numerous occasions, according to Ferrazzi, holy helpers freed her from men intent on violating her purity and from the Devil's assaults. In other instances, such as the "miraculous" birth of her sister, divine intervention modified the conditions of her subjection just enough to make possible her obedience to earthly superiors.

During the eighteen years between the death of her parents and her

tique?" in *Esperienza religiosa e scritture femminili tra Medioevo ed età moderna,* ed. Marilena Modica Vasta (Palermo: Bonnano, 1992), pp. 135–51.

24. Trial Record, Sentence (1 September 1665), separately paginated, fol. 2r.

establishment of a house for "girls in danger," Ferrazzi spent a prolonged adolescence under the surveillance of lay protectors/superiors: her uncle, Antonio and Ippolita Maffei, Andriana Cuccina, Modesta Salandi, and Marietta Cappello. In their homes she held a status somewhere between daughter and servant. Perhaps the most telling sign of her subordination to these protectors was Cappello's power to change her name.

Furthermore, from the time of the plague until the end of her life, Ferrazzi was subjugated to a succession of clerical superiors, her confessors. These priests exerted power over what they and she considered the most important part of her being, her soul; they controlled her access to the sacraments and to eternal life. Acting in the name of God, they could and did order her to despise and humiliate herself. For the most part insensitive and obsessed with their power, they sometimes fought over her and kicked her around "like a ball," as she put it. In this game, they set the rules and could arbitrarily change them.

Once she was denounced to the Inquisition, Ferrazzi came under the control of still other superiors, the inquisitor and his colleagues. These men had the power to determine where and how she spent the rest of her earthly life. They also exerted control over the image she had crafted for herself and projected to the public—a self-construction that had enabled her to rise above her station and find a place for herself in the world as a respected single woman providing a valuable social service.

PRETENSE

The Venetian Holy Office charged and eventually convicted Ferrazzi of "pretense of sanctity." This category of heresy had been articulated in the sixteenth century by Spanish inquisitors investigating *beatas*, "semi-religious" women who made informal, nonbinding vows to live chastely and austerely in the world. In the mid–1630s it finally made its way into manuals of procedure used in tribunals of the Roman Inquisition. The concept was variously termed *affettata, finta, pretesa,* or *simulata santità* ("assumed," "feigned," "claimed/ pretended," or "simulated holiness"). Its meaning cannot be fully grasped unless one realizes that in Italian the word cluster *santo/santa/santità* has two connotations that are represented in English by different words: "holy/holiness" and "saint/sanctity." Ferrazzi and others were charged not merely with feigning holy behavior but also with passing themselves off as "living saints." According to inquisitors, they claimed to be favorites of God who received revelations; merited special divine privileges, such as living on communion alone and bearing the wounds of Christ's Passion; and performed miracles. After they died, prosecutors feared, such specious marks of divine favor might win them an undeserved place among the officially recognized (beatified or canonized) spiritual heroes and heroines of the Catholic pantheon.[25]

By framing the phenomenon in this way, canon lawyers and theologians were implicitly rejecting the possibility that people who went into trances and exhibited extraordinary somatic signs and behaviors had been deluded by the Devil. This may seem like a great intellectual leap forward, and in one respect it was. Because Iberian and Italian inquisitors from the late sixteenth century on declined to take seriously the hypothesis that witchcraft was a conspiracy with the Devil, southern Europe never experienced the "witch craze" that afflicted transalpine Europe and North America.[26] Official skepticism about the role of the Devil in human behavior, however, had negative effects on some spiritually inclined women and men in territories where inquisitions operated. If the Devil could not have inspired them, the authorities reasoned, then they must be held responsible for fabricating, consciously and deliberately, evidence of a holiness they did not in fact possess.

Why did inquisitors assume that people like Ferrazzi must be faking, that they could not possibly be genuine "saints"? For one thing, like all early modern Europeans they were preoccupied with the widespread theory and practice of simulation and dissimulation: pretending to be what one was not, concealing one's real identity and convictions.[27] The notion of disingenuous self-fashioning to convey a false impression of holiness, mentioned in passing by Machiavelli in *The Prince*, achieved its most famous literary formulation in Molière's comedy *Tartuffe*, which dates from the same decade as Ferrazzi's trial. Furthermore, intellectuals in this era inherited a profoundly misogynist and elitist intellectual tradition. Inquisitors and theologians of the sixteenth and seventeenth centuries believed that God seldom communicated directly with "little people," and almost never with

25. The essential point of reference is Gabriella Zarri, ed., *Finzione e santità tra medioevo ed età moderna* (Turin: Rosenberg and Sellier, 1991), especially the following essays: Adriano Prosperi, "L'elemento storico nelle polemiche sulla santità," pp. 88–118; and Albano Biondi, "L'inordinata devozione' nella *Prattica* del Cardinale Scaglia (ca. 1635)," pp. 306–25. See also Zarri's classic article, "Living Saints: A Typology of Female Sanctity in the Early Sixteenth Century," trans. Daniel Bornstein, in *Women and Religion in Medieval and Renaissance Italy*, ed. Daniel Bornstein and Roberto Rusconi (Chicago: University of Chicago Press, 1996), pp. 219–303.

26. See Giovanni Romeo, *Inquisitori, esorcisti e streghe nell'Italia della Controriforma* (Florence: Sansoni, 1990), pp. 25–85.

27. An obligatory reference is Stephen Greenblatt, *Renaissance Self-fashioning from More to Shakespeare* (Chicago: University of Chicago Press, 1980). For a wide-ranging discussion of dissimulation somewhat more pertinent to the case of Ferrazzi, see Perez Zagorin, *Ways of Lying: Dissimulation, Persecution, and Conformity in Early Modern Europe* (Cambridge, Mass.: Harvard University Press, 1990). Neither Greenblatt nor Zagorin, however, pays much attention to women.

"little women." A nun who went into rapture and received divine revelations and privileges—Teresa of Avila is the best known but by no means the only example—might be given some benefit of the doubt. An uneducated lay-woman of modest social extraction like Ferrazzi was prejudged guilty of pretense. Little or nothing that she said or did, or that supporters adduced in her behalf, could reverse that verdict.[28]

AFTERMATH

After exercising her privilege of mounting a defense, Ferrazzi was con-demned by the Inquisition on 1 September 1665 "as lightly suspect of her-esy, that is, of holding and believing that it is licit for a Catholic Christian to make herself considered a saint." She was sentenced to seven years in jail, assigned various "salutary penances,"[29] and prohibited forever from talking about divine favors supposedly bestowed on her and from taking in "girls in danger." Her defense attorneys immediately appealed her case to the Con-gregation of the Holy Office in Rome.[30]

Soon thereafter, Doge Domenico Contarini began putting pressure on the papal nuncio in Venice, Stefano Brancacci, to take up the ailing Fer-razzi's case directly with Pope Alexander VII.[31] During the next two years the bureaucratic wheels in Rome ground very slowly. On 22 October 1667, however, Brancacci informed the Doge that the Holy Office had decided to transfer Ferrazzi from prison to house arrest in the custody of the Bishop of Padua, Cardinal Gregorio Barbarigo, a Venetian patrician well acquainted with her and many of her patrons.[32] This modified incarceration ended early in 1669, when the Congregation of the Holy Office ordered her release and allowed her to return to Venice.[33] How Ferrazzi spent the last fifteen years

28. See Anne Jacobson Schutte, "Piccole donne, grandi eroine: Santità femminile, 'simulata' e 'vera,' nell'Italia della prima età moderna," in *Donne e fede: Santità e vita religiosa*, ed. Lucetta Scaraffia and Gabriella Zarri (Rome: Laterza, 1994), pp. 277–301; English translation forthcoming). This and all other issues addressed here will receive fuller treatment in my forthcoming book *Clipped Wings: Pretense of Sanctity, the Inquisition, and Gender in Early Modern Venice*.

29. These included daily recitation of prescribed prayers and confession at regular intervals to priests designated by the religious authorities.

30. Trial Record, Sentence, fols. 22v–23r, title page.

31. VaAS, Nunziatura di Venezia, 300 (minutes of letters from the papal secretary of state to the nuncio in Venice, 1660–66), fols. 273r, 284r–85r.

32. VaAS, Nunziatura di Venezia, 106 (register of letters in cipher between the papal secretary of state and nuncios in Venice, 16 July 1667–23 November 1669), fol. 96v. Gregorio Barbarigo (1625–97) was beatified in 1761 and canonized in 1960.

33. Trial Record, annotations on the last (unnumbered) leaf.

of her life the sources do not reveal. After suffering for nine days from "internal inflammation with severe lung congestion and a fever," she died on 17 January 1684. Maria Fantini, a merchant's widow and longtime friend, arranged for her burial in San Lio, the church where she had been baptized almost seventy-three years earlier.[34]

Since Inquisition trial transcripts were kept secret, Cecilia Ferrazzi's autobiography had no impact whatever on her contemporaries or future generations until it was published in 1990. Her abjuration and sentence, however, circulated in compilations of sentences for pretense of sanctity.[35] Through an English writer's use of such a manuscript, anglophone readers soon learned something about Ferrazzi. In his book *The Present State of the Republick of Venice* (1669), Jean Gailhard devoted several pages to "a widow (of a competent estate, according to her quality, but inferiour to her heart) named Signora Cecilia." Although his source was a compilation of Inquisition sentences, he gave the impression that Ferrazzi had been tried by a secular court. Inventing a deceased husband and completely ignoring her visions, he placed exclusive emphasis on how cruelly she treated her charges and how many of them—so he claimed—were impregnated by Venetian nobles. As Gailhard made perfectly clear, his purpose was not to tell the story of her life but rather to illustrate "that lust of the flesh which Reigns every where in *Venice*, where 'tis fulfilled by young and old of all Sexes in the way of fornication, adultery, incest, sodomy, etc., so that though they be great Politicians, they are bad Christians and moral livers."[36]

It is ironic but not particularly surprising that the only notice of Cecilia

34. VeAS, Provveditori alla Sanità, busta 892 (necrology for the year 1683/84).

35. Some collections focused on women and men who had engaged in sexual activity in the belief (or on the pretext) that since they had been assured of their salvation, they were incapable of committing sin. In the late seventeenth century this belief became the hallmark of a spiritual movement known as Quietism, which was promptly condemned and vigorously prosecuted by the Holy Office. It may be that compilations of sentences against Quietists served not only to guide inquisitors but also to titillate them and other readers (John Tedeschi, personal communication).

36. Jean Gailhard, *The Present State of the Republick of Venice, as to the Government, Laws, Forces, Riches, Manners, Customes, Revenue, and Territory of that Commonwealth, with a Relation of the Present War in Candia* (London: For John Starkey, 1669), pp. 169–71. Some twenty-five works by Gailhard, almost certainly a native of France who relocated in England, were published between 1659 and 1705. A year before writing about Ferrazzi, he had demonstrated close acquaintance with the operations of the Venetian Inquisition (Jean Gailhard, *The Present State of the Princes and Republicks of Italy, with Observations on Them* [London: For John Starkey, 1668], pp. 106–7). That his source of information about Ferrazzi was a compilation of sentences is shown by a digression having nothing to do with Venice that immediately follows his discussion of her: the story of the Neapolitan Giulia Di Marco, a Franciscan tertiary sentenced for pretense of sanctity in Rome in 1615 along with two male sexual partners (Gailhard, *Present State . . . Venice*, pp. 171–74).

Ferrazzi's trial committed to print during her lifetime was framed in such a lurid fashion. With her own version of her life before them, readers of the late twentieth century can look for other, more central themes in the career of this aspiring saint. And they can employ different criteria in determining whether or not she was the cynical pretender her prosecutors judged her to be.

NOTE ON THE TRANSLATION

Cecilia Ferrazzi's testimony and autobiography come to us as transcriptions of oral performances. Like most speakers untrained in rhetoric, Ferrazzi strung together clause after clause with participial phrases and the conjunction *and*. In the original, each paragraph is a single sentence. To enhance comprehension while preserving something of the original flavor, I have broken up and reorganized many sentences, but I have tried not to betray the speaker by transmuting her speech into speciously elegant prose. The level of English diction chosen is informal; contractions (nonexistent in Italian) serve to suggest the spontaneity of speech. Words within brackets clarify the antecedents of pronouns and other locutions and supply names keyed to the lists of persons and places given in the appendices. Italian terms resistant to translation are retained and are defined in the glossary.

Antonio da Venezia's hand presents few challenges. Cecilia Ferrazzi's syntax, however, is occasionally daunting. Lending her fine Italian eye and ear, Elissa Weaver helped me to negotiate several labyrinthine passages. I gratefully acknowledge her assistance. Thanks are due also to Daniel Bornstein, reader for the University of Chicago Press, who offered many excellent suggestions for improvements in phrasing.

TESTIMONY OF FERRAZZI PRECEDING
HER AUTOBIOGRAPHY

The Venetian Inquisition first met regarding Cecilia Ferrazzi on 7 May 1664, when its members questioned Chiara Bacchis about the written denunciation she had submitted. Over the next few weeks, following the customary procedure, they interrogated several witnesses named by Bacchis who shed light on Ferrazzi and her activities. Having decided that there was sufficient evidence to pursue the matter, they ordered the arrest and imprisonment of the suspect. On 12 June Ferrazzi was apprehended in her gondola on the Grand Canal and taken to the Inquisition's prison.[1] A week later she was brought into court for the first time.

FIRST INTERROGATION

[Thursday,] 19 June 1664. In the presence of the Most Excellent Procurator [Pietro] Morosini. Before the Most Illustrious and Most Reverend Apostolic Nuncio [Iacopo Altoviti], etc., and the Most Reverend Father Inquisitor General [Agapito Ugoni] and the Vicar [Bartolomeo Giera] of the Most Illustrious and Most Reverend Patriarch of Venice [Giovanni Francesco Morosini], a certain woman about fifty years old of ordinary stature wearing a black woolen dress and a silk shawl, and on her forehead a white veil covered by a black veil,[2] [was] led from the prisons. Having been read the oath, etc., and touching [the Gospel], etc., she was sworn in, etc.[3]

1. The Holy Office maintained its own jail, where Ferrazzi was incarcerated, near the church of San Giovanni in Bragora. Some suspects and defendants were held in the complex of state prisons just east of Palazzo Ducale. Both were within easy walking distance of the tribunal's headquarters at the chapel of San Teodoro, behind the ducal church of San Marco.

2. Ferrazzi's dress was made of *scotto*, a sort of gabardine. Except for the two veils, an individual touch for which she accounts in the third interrogation, she was attired in the normal fashion of mature Venetian women below the patrician class.

3. *Etc.* is an abbreviation for the rest of the standard introductory formula. In transcripts of

Asked her name, surname, place of birth, age, occupation, residence, and [marital] status, etc., she replied, "My name is Cecilia, daughter of the late Alvise Ferrazzi and of Maddalena Polis, his wife. I was born in Venice, and I don't know where my father came from, although I've heard he was from Bassano. And I was orphaned at the age of sixteen or seventeen, when my parents died of the plague here in Venice. I don't know how old I am, and I think I was baptized in San Lio or Santa Marina.[4] I was raised in my father's house until I was about eighteen. Then, when my parents died, I was put in the house of my uncle Defendi [Polis], with whom I stayed about six months or less. Because he planned to marry me to that same notary who drafted the power of attorney[5] and I didn't want to marry, I fled from his house into the church of Sant'Aponal, opposite his house, on a Sunday about an hour before nones, and that evening at about twenty-three hours[6] I went home and begged his pardon. That night he had a stroke, and since that man to whom they wanted to marry me was still in the house and my aunt [Margherita (or Marietta) Polis] died accidentally the very same day, I arranged with Signor [Francesco] Molin, who later died as doge, then president of the *contrada*, to put me in refuge with Signor Francesco [Antonio] Maffei, where I stayed about two years. Then they put me in safekeeping with Signora Andriana Cuccina, and I stayed there seven or eight years, and she took care of me like one of her own daughters.

"After that, that is, during the last two years I was with the Cuccina family, I was taken in hand by Signor [Giorgio] Polacco, vicar of the nuns; I confessed to him, and he was my spiritual director.[7] He put me in safekeeping in the convent of the Cappuccine until he determined otherwise because he said that he wanted to examine me, and also because that notary

---

trials conducted by the Venetian Inquisition during this period, opening and closing formulae and procedural statements are in Latin, the inquisitor's questions and the witnesses' answers in Italian.

4. Ferrazzi was baptized on 20 April 1609 in the parish of San Lio. Sometime before her brother Mattio Anzolo was baptized on 13 November 1611, the Ferrazzi family moved to the adjacent parish of Santa Marina (VeAP, Santa Marina, Battesimi 2). Ferrazzi's contemporaries in all social ranks were just as imprecise as she about their age—in part, perhaps, because in Catholic Europe until fairly recent times, annual personal celebrations took place on the feast day of the saint for whom a person was named, not on his or her own birthday.

5. The notary is unidentified. Ferrazzi's allusion to a power of attorney may mean that after her uncle's death, the notary took legal action to secure custody of her in order to bring about the promised marriage.

6. Ferrazzi and her contemporaries kept time by the canonical hours and the sun's movement: nones is 3 P.M.; twenty-three hours is an hour before sunset.

7. A spiritual director advised devout penitents, as well as administering the sacraments of confession and communion to them.

who claimed to be my fiance was still alive and there was concern about what he might do. I stayed with the Cappuccine for three or four months, and Signor Vicar Polacco assigned as my confessor the Carmelite Father Master Bonaventura [Pinzoni], who is still alive, and this was before Signor Polacco put me in the Cappuccine—five or six years before. When I was in the Cappuccine, he [Polacco] took me out and had me confessed by various others, and he confessed me himself, and he had me make a general confession.[8]

"When I came out of the Cappuccine, he [Polacco] put me in the Dominican *pinzochere* at San Martin, and I stayed there about a month, or fifteen or twenty days. And because so many people were coming [to see me], he urged me to have myself put in an underground room, and during those few days he had me exorcised by various men in his presence: by a father of San Giobbe [Raimondo da Venezia], one from Santo Stefano [Nicola Stoppa], and a confessor of the nuns of Santa Giustina [Giovanni Zogalli]. And the reason for the exorcisms was that everyone said that I lived on communion alone,[9] and that if I tried to eat, I didn't hold down the food. And for the same reason, becoming suspicious, he removed me from the charge of that Carmelite confessor.

"I let the said Signor Polacco know that I ate when I could but couldn't keep anything in my stomach, and I even vomited clots of blood. And I was born with this infirmity; I've almost always done that, and I'm seeing a doctor even now. And I go for a day or two without eating, drinking only large flasks of water," and she made a sign indicating a flask costing one or two lire. "And after that day or two has passed and I eat (because I must obey, although as far as I'm concerned, I'd prefer not to eat so as not to suffer), I almost immediately throw it up, painfully and sometimes with blood, and the harder I try to hold down the food, the more I vomit blood.

"When the convent of Santa Teresa first opened at San Nicolò, I went there, but then I discovered that I was suffering from the stone,[10] and therefore I had to leave in order to seek a cure for this malady; at that time its nature was unknown, but it was diagnosed during the medical treatments.

8. Upon taking charge of new confessands, spiritual directors usually had them make a general confession covering their entire lives.

9. That is, taking no nourishment except the communion wafer dipped in wine. On this phenomenon, see Rudolph M. Bell, *Holy Anorexia* (Chicago: University of Chicago Press, 1985); and Fulvio Tomizza, *Heavenly Supper: The Story of Maria Janis*, trans. Anne Jacobson Schutte (Chicago: University of Chicago Press, 1991).

10. Bladder stones, a very common malady in the early modern period, are now known to be linked to dietary deficiencies.

And I passed stones this big."[11] To explain, she added, "Some as large as a little nut, others bigger, and even as big as a hen's egg. After the treatment I took a house at San Lorenzo and had with me two girls from Bassano, now dead, who looked after me. And little by little, first I was given a small child who was going around begging, then another, then another, and so on, so that when I left there, where I stayed seven to eight years (no, five or six), I had one hundred twenty girls, with whom I went to San Giovanni Evangelista, and I stayed there to govern these girls, who increased in number. And from there, because of the bad water, I moved to Cannaregio, where I stayed about two years, and since on account of the increased number I couldn't remain there, the house at Sant'Antonio in which the nobleman [Domenico] Ruzzini lived was purchased by the noblemen [Francesco] Vendramin and [Sebastiano] Barbarigo, and there I've lived until the time I was put in jail."

Then she added voluntarily,[12] "While talking about my illness, we've left out some things, namely that when I left the previously mentioned *pinzochere*, Signor Polacco put me in the home of a certain noblewoman Pizzamano, who suffered from that ugly sickness,[13] near San Barnaba, and I was not given anything to eat or drink, nor did I want anyone to know about it, not even my own sister, who is Sister Maria Ventura at Santa Teresa. And instead of a mattress, I slept on a box like this"—and she made a sign—"about two *braccia* long and three-quarters of a *braccio* wide. And there I was, without being given anything to eat or drink, for about fifty days, suffering from hemorrhages. It's true that the theologians who came to examine me sometimes brought me some biscuits and a little fruit, particularly Father [Michiel] Stella of the Frari, who confessed the nuns of San Lorenzo. And I almost despaired and let the Devil take my life. And things to eat were brought or sent to me almost every day, and I ate what I could, but I vomited it up as usual. And the one who sent the provisions was Father Stella, who during the week he was confessing the nuns sent that noblewoman something to give me. After fifty days, because it was being said that I had died, a *pinzochera* came from the Carmini to see me, and she found me in a very bad state on that box, and therefore she ran to report to my sister, who came around two hours after sunset, contrary to my [vow of] obedience to Signor Polacco, who didn't want anyone to visit me.

11. At this point, as Holy Office notaries usually state explicitly, she must have gestured to indicate how big the stone was.

12. That is, not in response to a question.

13. Epilepsy.

"Then I had a temptation that almost drove me to desperation, and it was this. One day around noon, and it was the Vigil of All Saints,[14] while I was being very carefully watched, I saw coming into my room—just as I see you gentlemen now, for it was neither a dream nor a vision—a number of people, twenty or thirty, dressed in black like the Company of San Fantin, who carried a crucifix as large as a man, and laying it on the ground, they sang over it, but I couldn't understand what they were saying, even though I heard them singing. And I turned toward the crucifix, begging pardon and praying for my soul, and that Christ bowed His head as if He didn't want to listen to me. Then, in tears, I began praying to Him, fearing that I was unworthy of His hearing my prayers, and I saw Him detach His arm from the cross two or three times, making a gesture of rebuffing me and saying no, whereupon I judged myself practically abandoned by God and in a state of desperation. At the hour of vespers this crucifix and the company disappeared, and at around twenty-two hours[15] I saw a hermit coming into the room in a gray garment resembling a hairshirt with a great big beard and a hood over his forehead—all hairy, even his hands—with a breviary under his arm and a rope belt. And when he said that he had come from God, I rejoiced, and he told me that for thirty-three years he had not laid eyes on a living soul and that he had come to help me go away to do penance.[16] And I replied that I couldn't leave unless I were dispensed from obedience. He wanted me to depart right away with him, but I put him off for a week[17] until Father Stella finished confessing the nuns. For that entire week he stayed with me day and night kneeling on a prayer stool with his back to me leafing through that breviary, and he talked and talked, but I never heard what he said. And in that period of time I don't remember whether I ate or drank because it was as though I were dead, dead, with the blood running down me in buckets.[18]

At the end of the week that *pinzochera* came, and it was the evening of the Vigil of All Saints, and to tell the honest truth she was sent by that Carmelite confessor who'd been prohibited from [seeing] me, and he went to inform my sister. And that very evening at the door on the street, she

14. 31 October. In Ferrazzi's vision a week went by, but the actual elapsed time seems to have been a few hours.

15. Vespers: about 6 P.M.; twenty-two hours would have been not long afterward at this time of year.

16. In this context, to flagellate oneself.

17. Literally, eight days, a common way of indicating a week in Italian.

18. As a result of beating herself.

sent her mother to fetch my sister, for that *pinzochera*, as superior of her convent, had to be there during the night. When my sister arrived, the woman left. And at midnight the hermit began insisting that since the week I had taken was over, I had to leave with him, and he wanted me to renounce the name of Mary and curse obedience, to stamp my feet on the ground while saying, 'I curse obedience! Damned obedience!' And although during that week I had been consoled by his staying in my room, now I realized that he was the Devil and not a person sent by God.

"Then I took a bunch of keys, and despite the fact that he wanted me to throw myself down from a balcony in that room, which was high and he made it appear low, I took a bunch of rusty keys attached to the wall and called on the Blessed Virgin. While beating me and dragging me to and fro, he grabbed me by the braids and made me hit my head violently on the walls on both sides [of the room], splattering the walls with blood. I ended up with my head, or rather my scalp, peeled, for my braids remained [in his hand] and the hair never grew back, and thus I'm bald now. While this was going on, my sister, who had been asleep, woke up, saying that she'd heard me shout, and already the Devil had disappeared, having heard me invoke the names of Jesus and Mary.

"The following day, after Monsignor Patriarch [Federico] Corner had sent some gentlewomen and others, Monsignor Polacco arrived, and he took me to the convent of Santa Maria Maggiore so that they would take me in, and because they didn't want to, he yelled loudly, 'I'm giving you a saint and you don't want her!'" And while this was being written down, she added voluntarily, "But it isn't true, sir, because I'm a sinner. The next morning the Lord Cardinal sent me back and, by means of a note in his own hand, arranged my acceptance by those mothers. Once they had taken me in, they made so much of me that I had difficulty refraining from the sin of vainglory."[19]

And since the hour was late, having sworn and signed the transcript and having taken the oath of silence, the person under examination was dismissed.

[signed] I, Cecilia.

---

19. On this incident, which took place in 1637–38, see the text of Ferrazzi's autobiography, below. It is discussed fully in Anne Jacobson Schutte, "Discernment and Discipline: Giorgio Polacco and Religious Women in Early Modern Italy," in *Culture and Self in Renaissance Europe*, ed. William J. Connell (Berkeley: University of California Press, forthcoming).

At the next meeting of the Holy Office on 23 June, the inquisitor interrogated Florena di Antonio Forni, a nineteen-year-old Venetian woman who had lived for several years in Ferrazzi's house at Sant'Antonio di Castello before escaping a month earlier to the home of her sister and brother-in-law. Florena reiterated and expanded on damaging allegations furnished by previous witnesses. Then Ferrazzi was brought back into court.

SECOND INTERROGATION

[Monday,][20] 23 June 1664. [The members of the tribunal in attendance, listed at the beginning of this day's session, were the same as on 19 June.] Led from the prisons, the aforesaid lady Cecilia, etc.; the oath was administered to her, etc., while she touched, etc., swore, etc.

Asked whether she needed to say anything in this case, she replied, "Nothing else occurs to me except that what I've done, I've done in order to do God's will, and for my soul and those of the girls whom I've governed."

And ordered to continue the account of her life after she was received by the nuns of Santa Maria Maggiore, she replied, "I should say first that it had slipped my mind that while I was in the house of Signora Modesta [Salandi], a noblewoman, Marietta Cappello, came to remove me from Signor Polacco's hands and took me to her house, changing my name so that it wouldn't be known where I was, and I was called Chiara, while at baptism I was named Cecilia Corona. [This was] because the said Signor Polacco kicked me around like a ball, making me go here and there, and that caused murmuring among the people, for some said that I was a saint, others that I was possessed, but my honor wasn't impugned the way it is now, when it's being said that I've had children. Signor Polacco came to the grate at Santa Maria Maggiore and wept and drenched three or four handkerchiefs, telling me, 'I've betrayed you, assassinated you! I know I've done wrong, but bear with me, because you are possessed.' And all the nuns of Santa Maria Maggiore were called in, and in their presence he said those things to me, and he went so far as to have me given communion with an unconsecrated wafer, telling me, 'Come on, go into ecstasy because you're possessed!' And for this reason the said Signora Cappello took me away from Signora Modesta. And I forgot to say that when that priest—I don't know who he was—gave me that unconsecrated wafer, he also gave me a shove that made me fall backward over a wooden clog, which hurt me so

20. The Holy Office normally met on Tuesday and Thursday, and occasionally on Saturday mornings. Sessions held on other days indicate a press of business in this and other cases on the docket.

badly that I had to be put in the care of a barber.[21] And this was in a little chapel outside the cloister after I had left the said monastery and gone to the house of the said Signora Modesta. For nine years I stayed with the said Cappello, treated like her own daughter, nor did she let anyone see me. She had me eat at her table, and in every way I was treated like one of her daughters, Cecilia, and we always went out together, too. She even took me to Este."

While this was being written down, she volunteered, "All during those nine years I confessed to Alvise Zonati, chaplain in San Severo, confessor of that noblewoman, and that was arranged by the said Signora Marietta and the confessor, nor did I know what my own will was, because they ordered everything contrary to my will, and I obeyed. After this I went to my sister's, then to San Lorenzo, then to San Giovanni Evangelista, then to Cannaregio, and then to Castello."

Asked whether she knew or could guess the reason why she has been held in this Holy Office, she responded, "I don't know, nor can I imagine, except for what I heard before I was imprisoned, because it was being said of me that I had a relationship with someone from the Lion household, some [said] one, others another, and that I gave birth to and killed a child[22]—that I wore gold overskirts, and pearls around my neck, had myself adored and my feet kissed, dressed as a confessor and administered confession and communion, and when they [the girls] came out of the confessional, I grabbed and shook them for the sins confessed to me—things, however, which are all completely false, for I'm as clear and pure as a crystal and a virgin, too, and just as I am, so are all the others.[23] They were saying, too, that I turned three or four of those girls over to whores, who gave me purses of gold, and also that I claimed that it was God's providence that supported me—which is false as well. But since I must tell the truth, I think it's possible—although I don't want anyone to know it and would rather be walled up—that the said Signor Polacco spread the word that I had the stigmata[24] and that I lived on communion alone, even though I pitied the poor man, who must have done it for a good purpose, as I believe, because he also said that I might have been tricked by the Devil.

21. In the early modern era, barbers rather than physicians performed most minor surgical operations.

22. Several witnesses later asserted that the man in question was Bortolomio Ferlini, steward of the Lion household, who was alive at the time of the trial but was never called to testify.

23. "Crystal . . . others": translation based on a conjectural reading of a difficult passage; by "the others," Ferrazzi clearly means the girls under her supervision.

24. Wounds like those inflicted on Christ during His Passion.

"And to explain the matter as it was, I'll say that as I was being taken to Mirano by Signora Andriana Cuccina, either on account of the rattling of the carriage or for some other reason, I spilled a great deal of blood that stuck my shirt to my waist, which before then was all cut up, whether because of the Devil's beatings or because of natural defect or infirmity I don't know. I know that I certainly had battles with the Devil, and I give my confessors permission to talk about it so that the truth will come out.[25]

"Well, then, when I had arrived at Mirano with that lady, they made me retire into a room, where, having locked myself in with a big chain, I began to undress, and when I took off my shirt, pieces of skin came off my waist, all dripping blood. Now while I was in that painful state, I noticed that opposite a window in the room there was a little chapel with a crucifix in it. Having pulled the shirt from my skin but keeping my dress on (for I never undress, since I sleep in my shirt and a white bodice), I turned in anguish from the pain to implore that crucified Christ to clothe me in the love of His Passion and allow me to feel some of His pain, that is, a bit of it. And then I saw something like a fire, divided into five rays like lines from His wounds, detach itself from that crucifix. And standing with my arms extended in the form of a cross, I felt those rays strike my hands, feet, and ribs, and I felt very great pains, which I feel even now most of the time, at certain times in particular. And I fell to the ground as if dead (since I was then on my knees in prayer, I fell over onto my right side), so that even though there was a knock at the door, as I learned later, I didn't hear a thing.

"But then Father Master Bonaventura of the Carmine, at that time provincial of the order and formerly my confessor, turned up by chance; I don't know whether God or the Devil sent him at that moment, since he had been away for a month on a visitation. And when he arrived at that house, Signora Andriana told him that I was in that room, locked in, and that when she'd knocked at the door, I hadn't responded, and since she knew that I was unwell, she wondered whether something terrible had happened to me. I don't know how the door was opened, but I heard that father say, 'Cecilia, obedience!' I couldn't move because I was lying on the ground on my side. But I revived at the word *obedience* and managed to get up, and the confessor said to me, 'Daughter, hide yourself and have patience, don't suffer, for these are cold sores which come like this.' I withdrew with the said Signora Andri-

---

25. That is, she releases her confessors from the seal of the confessional, the complete confidentiality that (at least in theory) shielded everything discussed by a penitent and confessor during administration of the sacrament of penance. Since Ferrazzi and her spiritual directors had frequent conversations outside the confessional, the formal limitation on what they could tell the inquisitor meant relatively little in this case.

ana, and because I still felt great pain even in my feet, I took off my stockings in her presence, and one could see that my feet were badly injured and swollen, with wounds and blood. Signora Andriana medicated me, that is, she helped me and hid me as best she could.

"When I came back four or five days later from Este, where we went after Mirano, I was put by Signor Polacco in the convent of the Cappuccine, as planned before my departure, and there inside the convent I was treated for my wounds—that is, [the ones] on the hands and feet, but I begged them not to medicate my side so that my waist wouldn't be seen. For every so often I bled, since my hands and feet were pierced from one side to the other. I don't know whether they were actually pierced; I felt pain on both sides and there were marks and blood on both sides.[26] This treatment lasted ten or twenty days—I don't know exactly, sir—in the convent of the Cappuccine. And even after I was cured, the scars remained, so in my prayers I begged God to send me any other kind of mortification rather than this one of leaving me with the scars for people to point at. I feel the pain especially on Friday—but listen, sir, I believe that it was a temptation of the Devil, and God forbid, sir, for the Devil disguises himself as an angel of light,[27] and that's what I've told everyone."

Asked whether she had shown anyone these wounds or signs, she replied, "I showed them to Signora Caterina Fasana, a *dimessa* who came occasionally to see me. When she tried to kiss my hand, I hit her in the face, and at that time I was sick in bed at Signora Marietta Cappello's. And when I went through the city and heard people say, 'Look, there's the holy woman with the stigmata,' I addressed myself to the Lord and said, 'Lord, You who gave them to me, I beg You to hide me, or give me patience.' And therefore, even in my house and other places, when I heard myself praised, I dismissed it, saying that I was a sinner."

And since the hour was late and the Holy Tribunal had by this time been in session four hours, [the person being examined] was dismissed, etc.

[signed] I, Cecilia.

---

26. Translation based on a conjectural reading of a difficult passage: by conceding that she is not certain about the piercing, Ferrazzi prudently qualifies her previous insinuation that God had indeed given her one of his highest signs of favor, the stigmata, and that they had not been imprinted by the Devil.

27. 2 Corinthians 11:14, one of two main proof texts for distinguishing between divine and diabolical inspiration, which Ferrazzi's spiritual advisers must have cited to her many times. (The other is 1 John 4:1.)

Between 23 June and 3 July the Holy Office convened three times. On 27 June the tribunal entered into the record copies of letters and reports documenting Ferrazzi's "time of troubles" in late 1637 and early 1638, when Giorgio Polacco, vicar of the nuns, at the order of his superior, Patriarch Federico Corner, conducted an investigation of her alleged stigmata and other evidence of her apparent holiness.[28] *On 30 June and 1 July the inquisitor questioned Florena Forni again and interrogated four other inmates of Ferrazzi's establishments. During this period the Holy Office dispatched Andrea Vescovi, chancellor of the tribunal, to Sant'Antonio di Castello to inspect and furnish a report on two paintings mentioned by several witnesses. At its next meeting, on 3 July, a neighbor of Ferrazzi was interrogated before she herself was summoned to testify for the third time.*

THIRD INTERROGATION

[Thursday,] 3 July 1664. In the presence of the Most Excellent Lord Procurator Morosini. Before the Most Illustrious and Most Reverend Lord Apostolic Nuncio and the Most Reverend Father Inquisitor General and the Vicar of the Patriarch, the said Cecilia [was] led from the prisons, etc.; the oath was administered to her, etc., while she touched, etc., swore, etc.

Asked whether she had anything she wished to say, she replied, "No, surely not, except what I've said and am prepared to confirm."

And told to think carefully, and if she recognized herself guilty of some other crime, to tell about it freely before she was questioned in detail, for by doing so she would gain greater mercy from this Holy Office, she replied, "I certainly have nothing else on my conscience to report."

Asked whether she had enemies, and if so to name them and explain the cause of the enmity, she replied, "I have as enemies several prostitutes who have given me their daughters in custody. Because I don't want to release them, for they would get into trouble, [these women] hate me and have decided to say bad things about me. But I don't know who they are because there are many of them.[29] Besides, a noblewoman hates me: the widow [Isabella Zen Barbaro] of a nobleman of the Barbaro family who was in the government, and now one of her stepsons [Zorzi Barbaro] is married, [and he has] two young daughters, one nine and the other ten, whose names

28. VeAS, Sant'Ufficio, busta 112 (hereafter cited as Trial Record), fols. 27r–29v and two unnumbered leaves.

29. Ferrazzi must have known that the prostitute Chiara Perini Bacchis, a native of Bassano living in Padua, had filed a suit with a civil magistracy, the Avogadori di Comun, to get her two daughters and a niece released from Ferrazzi's house at Sant'Antonio di Castello. She could probably have guessed that Bacchis and a younger Venetian woman, Chiara Garzoni (formerly Ferrazzi's second in command and now a competitor running a house for "girls in danger"), had denounced her to the Inquisition.

I don't remember; I recall one, named Chiaretta.[30] I thought everyone liked me, but now I realize that they wish me ill, above all those who have daughters in my care. Another person who hates me is a certain [Giovan Paolo] Spinelli, a *cittadino* of Venice who goes around begging; he lives at San Girolamo, and he has a son who poisoned himself at the Jesuits'.[31] Besides these, I can't think of any others. And all this is because I didn't want to let [the girls] hang out the windows but kept them in seclusion in honor of God.

Asked who were her confessors after Signor Polacco, she replied, "Signor Father Alvise Zonati for nine years. After him came Signor Father Antonio Grandi, *pievano* of San Giovanni di Rialto, and he confessed me and all the girls at San Giovanni Evangelista. In that same place, after the said Don Antonio, came one who confessed and still confesses the hermitesses of San Marcuola, who's called Father Zuanne the Slav [Giovanni Andreis], and he confessed only the girls but not me because I didn't want it even though he did, except for an occasional reconciliation,[32] for I was confessing to the said *pievano*. And I told that same *pievano* everything, including the way the said Father Zuanne went about confessing the girls and the great desire he had to confess me as well. And the said *pievano* told me, 'It's good for you if you don't like him,'[33] and I sent him away."

Asked how she knew about the said Father Zuanne's manner of confessing, she replied, "Because I saw [the girls] engaging in various kinds of simulated holiness, undertaking certain fasts, staying up at night and saying the Rosary on their knees, and performing types of penitence I didn't like. During my life I've had only five other confessors assigned to me: that is, first, a certain priest called Pisani; second, Father Bonaventura the Carmelite; Signor Polacco (but he doesn't count because he confessed and examined me when I was about to become a nun);[34] third, Father Alvise Zonati; fourth,

30. Ferrazzi means that Zorzi Barbaro had placed his daughters in her house at Sant'Antonio di Castello.

31. Presumably the boy was a boarder at the Jesuit college.

32. For confessions that immediately precede taking communion, Ferrazzi uses the word *reconciliation*, which she and her contemporaries distinguished from longer sacramental confessions, on the one hand, and conferences with one's spiritual director outside the confessional, on the other.

33. Translation based on a conjectural reading of a difficult passage. Grandi, as quoted by Ferrazzi, seems to be saying that an uncongenial confessor is better for the soul than an overly sympathetic one.

34. Evidently Ferrazzi, who was in her late twenties at this point, still hoped to be admitted to some convent, either Santa Teresa or Santa Maria Maggiore. Her persistent illness and the questionable source of her spiritual inspiration explain why no convent ever accepted her as a novice.

the aforementioned signor *pievano* of San Giovanni; and fifth, the Jesuit fathers. And the first of these was Father [Girolamo] Chiaramonte, who sought to liberate me from deception by having me recount the entire course of my life. And this father confessor, to whom the signor *pievano* sent me, told me that I should have patience and remain humble and that he intended to go to Monsignor the Patriarch and assure him that I had never given credence to what had happened during my life. And I've been sought out many times by confessors, nuns, and secular persons, and I've told them all that I'm indeed a virgin and that God protect us all from the Devil's tricks. After Father Chiaramonte, to whom I confessed for four or five months before he went away—and he also confessed a few of the more spiritual girls in [the house in] Cannaregio—Father [Daniele] Bartoli came to confess me for about three months. I recounted my whole life to him, too, and he told me that I had done well and must continue to abhor these things and mustn't talk about them. Then came Father [Paolo] Casati, who confessed me for about three years while he was in Venice, and when he was out of town, I confessed to another Jesuit father, I don't recall who. Now I remember, it was Father [Camillo] Rodengo. And when he went to Padua, I confessed to the Jesuit Father Alessandro Zampi. All these fathers gave me advice along the same lines as Father Chiaramonte's."

Asked who the girls' confessors were, she replied, "The same ones who confessed me confessed the girls, too, for where the head made her confessions, there the members confessed also. And after the number of girls grew, [the confessors] came in pairs, and they finished in one day, and this has been for the past two or three years."

Asked how long it had been since she had gone with her girls to live in Castello, she replied, "It has been about three or four years."

Asked whether any Capuchin had ever confessed the said girls, she replied, "No, sir, never."[35]

Asked who was the first Jesuit to confess her girls, she replied, "The first was Father Chiaramonte, who confessed a few of them as I've said, and then Father Bartoli, who confessed some of them. Then Father [Alessandro] Boselli came to confess the girls; I didn't confess [to him] in the house, but occasionally in his church, the Gesuiti."

Asked whether she had ever previously been investigated or incarcerated, by either the Holy Office or other tribunals, she replied, "No, never. It is true, however, as I said, that the Father Inquisitor [Clemente Ricetti]

---

35. Here the inquisitor begins to probe the issue of whether Ferrazzi, disguised with a hood as a Capuchin friar, had administered confession to her girls.

came to Santa Maria Maggiore, the convent where I was, and interrogated me about these things."

Asked whether, when the Father Inquisitor talked with her, anyone wrote down the questions and responses, [she] replied, "Yes, sir, there at the grate, but this took only a quarter of an hour, and he left saying only, 'Bear patiently with this lord whom God has given you.'"[36]

Asked who was this lord whom God had given her, she replied, "It was Monsignor Polacco, vicar of the nuns."

Asked whether the Father Inquisitor said anything to her about the occurrences in her life (that is, revelations, visions, ecstasies, and stigmata), she replied, "He just asked what had happened during my life, and I told him, and he said nothing else except that I should have patience with this lord. I'd forgotten that Signor Dr. Zogalli was also my confessor, assigned to me by Monsignor the Most Illustrious Patriarch, just as I've had all the other confessors under obedience. To tell the truth, this Monsignor Zogalli always treated me with abhorrence and disdain, berating me even in the presence of other people and of the nuns of Santa Giustina, whose confessor he was, because he must have been afraid of me, and I of him. When I was called before Monsignor the Most Illustrious Patriarch, he commanded that I go and confess to Signor Zogalli and leave Signor Alvise, and he gave Signor Zogalli license to report to him everything I said about my life. Promptly obeying, I went to find him and confessed to him. He mistreated and mortified me in a disdainful manner, and I wept and thanked God all day long because this flesh felt the effects."

And after this was written, she added, recollecting, "I was also being troubled by physical ailments. He told me that these visions and stigmata of mine were all temptations, and I confessed them as such."

Asked for what reason the said Zogalli was afraid of her and she of him, she replied, "Because he was young, and—my dear sir, I'm speaking freely—everyone should be afraid, for he who doesn't fear falls. And because he treated me strangely, and this was known in Ca' Lion and elsewhere, Signori Barbarigo and Lion went to Monsignor the Most Illustrious Patriarch in order to remove me from his [Zogalli's] hands, and they told him that he [Zogalli] had tested and grilled me enough. And I was assigned another confessor."

36. The documents concerning this investigation inserted into the Trial Record do not include a transcript of Ferrazzi's interview with the inquisitor.

Asked whether in her place in Castello anyone had her portrait painted by an artist,[37] she replied, "Listen, sir, if I hadn't been ordered to have my portrait painted, sir, I wouldn't have done it, God forbid, and I did it weeping. Listen, sir. My portrait was painted twice, once at San Lorenzo in my house at the initiative of the nobleman Sebastiano Barbarigo, who is now dead, by Signor [Nicolò] Renieri the painter—that is, it was begun in my house, where the painter came twice, and then he took it to his house. And on the pretext of having me come to visit two of the painter's daughters, in two sittings they finished the head. And since I didn't want to go there again, they had me take off what I was wearing and put on something else I had with me.[38] When I became ill, I said that I didn't want that painting seen, and I had it removed, and it was taken by the *pievano* of San Giovanni di Rialto to his house. And my dear sir, my image was captured against my will. And then it was brought back to my house, by whom I don't know, and turned over to me partly finished. The subject was dressed in the clothes I ordinarily wear, with a black headcovering, and without the little black and white veils I wear on my head now because I have no hair. And this is the one that, if Your Reverend Paternity will go to my place, you will see hung in my room, altered to resemble St. Teresa.

"The other portrait of me was done by Don Armano [Ermanno Stroiffi], who if I'm not mistaken came to [my house in] Cannaregio with Father Zuanne the Slav, the aforementioned confessor of the girls, who as confessor of the place, taking pleasure in paintings, ordered that I let my portrait be painted. Thus, after much begging and weeping, I agreed, and in two mornings he finished the head. And when I moved house, these two paintings were brought to Castello, and for a long time they were in the attic. About six months ago, on the arrival of Don Giacinto [Cornacchioli], an old foreign priest who says Mass in our chapel, I asked him to retouch these two paintings in such a way that no one would know it was I. And he turned one into St. Teresa and the other into the Virgin of the Arrows,[39] but he didn't alter the face. Then, to please the girls and have pictures in the house, the one representing the Virgin was placed in the choir and the St. Teresa in my room."

37. On the portraits, see Anne Jacobson Schutte, "'Questo non è il ritratto che ho fatto io': Painters, the Inquisition, and the Shape of Sanctity in Seventeenth-Century Venice," in *Florence and Italy: Studies in Honour of Nicolai Rubinstein*, ed. Peter Denley and Caroline Elam (London: Westfield College, 1988), pp. 419–31.

38. Ferrazzi's use of the plural indicates that the portrait was a collaborative project begun by Renieri and carried on by his daughters. Presumably they asked that she leave her clothes so that they could use them to finish the portrait in the sitter's absence.

39. The Virgin of the Seven Sorrows, surrounded by seven arrows.

And because the hour was late, the person being interrogated was dismissed and sent back to her place [in prison], with silence imposed, etc., and she signed, etc.

[signed] Jesus, Cecilia

Between the third and fourth interrogations of Ferrazzi the transcript records no further developments in the case.

FOURTH INTERROGATION

[Tuesday,] 8 July 1664. In the presence of the Most Excellent Lord Alvise Zusto. Before the Most Reverend Father Inquisitor General and the Auditor of the Most Illustrious and Most Reverend Apostolic Nuncio and the Vicar of the Most Illustrious and Most Reverend Lord Patriarch, etc., the said lady Cecilia [was] led from the prisons, etc.; the oath was administered to her, etc., while she touched, etc., swore, etc.

Asked whether she had anything to say of her own accord about her case, she replied, "I can't think of anything else to say, only that I forgot to mention two other confessors to whom I confessed with permission from Monsignor the Most Illustrious Patriarch: Father Orandi [Giovanni Battista Aldrovandi], now provincial of the Jesuit fathers, who also confessed the girls; and Father [Giacomo Antonio] Corner of the Carità for five to six months, since he lived near Signora Marietta Cappello, who was his penitent; and by Father Orandi for six to seven months, while Father Casati was away from Venice, at Sant'Antonio di Castello."

While this was being written down, the Most Illustrious and Most Reverend Nuncio arrived.

"I didn't tell Father Orandi much about my past life, little or nothing, but rather what happened to me day by day—that is, what I needed for myself and my girls, and particularly about some girl tempted by the Devil and her thoughts about vanity or liberty or other similar things put into her head by the Devil. To Father Corner I recounted the entire course of my life, for then I was being talked about all over the city, some saying good things and others bad, and to unburden my conscience I told him everything in order to justify myself.[40] And during that time I confessed to and took communion from him almost every day, even though I didn't seek this and called myself unworthy of it."

---

40. Translation based on a conjectural reading of a difficult passage. Ferrazzi appears to suggest that by confessing fully to Corner, she hoped to gain an ally who would seek to rebut the negative opinions about her that by this time were circulating widely in Venice.

Asked what the said father told her about the things she recounted about her life, she replied, "He said this: that it was temptation and that I should keep myself low in my nothingness, as I always have, and that the Devil could dress himself as an angel of light."

Asked whether she had ever had visions of the Most Blessed Virgin or the angels or the saints, whether she had conversed with them or they with her, she replied, "Yes, sir, but look, I never believed them."

And having been told to recount particular instances (where, when, how often, in what circumstances, and in whose presence), she replied, "My dear sirs, I beg you not to make me say these things because I have never accepted them and I'd rather suffer than speak about them."

And told that the Holy Office had administered the oath to her so that she would tell the truth about everything, and that therefore she had to recount everything, for so the obedience she owed required, she replied, "Since you command me in the name of obedience, I'll talk. I was persecuted from the beginning of my life, that is from about five or six years old, and I went on like that for fifteen to sixteen years without telling anyone anything that was happening to me. Then I started telling the Carmelite father confessor because he asked me, and this was that Father Bonaventura assigned to me by Signor Polacco. I was born infirm, so to speak, and before the age of seven I got three or four sets of new teeth, and although my mother wanted to pull them out for me, she couldn't.[41] I suffered considerably from great bodily pains, and while I was suffering, I saw a beautiful creature arrive to visit and console me."

Asked who this creature was, whether male or female, of what age, what appearance it had, or what did it appear or seem to her to be, where, when, during the day or at night, and how it was dressed when it appeared to her, and what it said, she replied, "It was a woman, young, so beautiful that the more I gazed at her the more lovely she seemed, in glowing garments I couldn't look at. She told me, 'I suffered for the love of God, for the love of my dear Son,' from which I inferred that She was the Blessed Virgin. How many times it happened I can't count: in my father and mother's house in all the rooms, whether I was sewing or sweeping or doing other household chores, She was before my eyes." And after this was written, she said, "Dear sirs, do me the favor of sending me either a confessor or anyone you want who'll write down everything I'll dictate to him, and I'll remember

41. Ferrazzi probably grew "supernumerary teeth" (duplicates or even triplicates of adult teeth), which sometimes appear between the ages of six and ten, particularly in the mouths of subjects who have suffered in infancy from high fevers (Hal M. Lippard, DDS, personal communication).

better and be less embarrassed, and then it can be taken to the Holy Office, and when the entire [manuscript] has been read in my presence, I'll confirm it."

Then the Most Holy Tribunal ruled that it was appropriate to make this opportunity available and selected for this office Father Antonio da Venezia, Reader [in theology] of the Order of Observant Friars Minor at the monastery of San Francesco della Vigna. This having been done, she was sent back to her place and signed, with silence imposed, etc.

[signed] Ceilia[42]

---

42. Ferrazzi's misspelled signature reveals her uncertain command of the written word, no doubt rendered even more tenuous by the stress of being interrogated.

AUTOBIOGRAPHY
OF
CECILIA FERRAZZI

In the name of the Lord and of His Mother, the Most Holy Virgin Mary. On [Wednesday,] 9 July 1664, in the prison of the Holy Inquisition of Venice.

I, Cecilia Ferrazzi, depose as the truth the things written below, which happened to me from the age of five until the present time.

From the moment I was born until this very hour, I've always been sick—and to be precise, the illness began to develop when I was five, with very great pains and loss of consciousness.

At the same age, one day when I was asleep on my mother's lap, I awoke very frightened and said to my mother that at that very moment they were killing my father. And just then a crowd of people brought him home covered with knife wounds but not badly injured because only his skin was cut. And I've heard this recounted by my mother several times, though I don't remember having told her because I was so young.

Around the same time there came upon me a very great desire to love and enjoy Blessed God, acquired from the good example and teaching of my mother, whom I heard reading books of devotion, especially the lives of male and female saints, and saying the Rosary with her children, all of us little. And when she realized that I had that feeling toward God, she isolated me from my brothers, letting me have very little to do with them, so I felt as if I were out of this world, for she didn't even allow me to associate with the wet nurse employed in the house.

As I grew from six to seven to eight, my bodily pains grew, too, with fits and fainting spells. And my mother had me dressed in dark blue in honor of St. Valentine, saying that such fits and pains were convulsions.[1] And to

---

1. Physiological psychologists link temporal lobe epilepsy with strong religious impulses and visionary experiences. Tempting as it may seem to label Ferrazzi an epileptic, her contemporar-

relieve me there appeared a beautiful creature in the form of a woman in a glowing dress that my eyes couldn't look at, who consoled me by saying that I must suffer these pains willingly for the love of God. From then on this young woman disappeared and returned both during the day and at night, once or twice a day and the same at night, and especially while I was in prayer reciting the Our Father and the Hail Mary and the Rosary, for these were the prayers I said in those days.

When I was twelve, despite the fact that I was unwell, my mother began to put me in charge of the housework. In [order to fulfill] this assignment, since I wasn't strong, I commended myself to the Most Holy Mother so that She would help me pay holy obedience to my mother and father. I offered myself to the Most Holy Mother Mary, begging that She give me grace to [gain] as much merit from serving my father as serving God, [from serving] my mother as [serving] the Most Holy Virgin, and [serving] my brothers as if they were angels and saints of paradise—although I was ashamed of serving my father and brothers, for it has always been my inclination to have nothing to do with men or even let them see me. And I tried to avoid my father and brothers as much as possible, retiring at night to say those few prayers, since during the day I was busy around the house.

And seeking to raise my brothers with the greatest possible purity and devotion, I delighted in talking with them of the greatness of Lord God. And a week before the feast days of male and female saints, I had them read their lives, inciting them to devotion toward them [the saints] so that they knelt with their bare knees on the ground and lashed themselves with whips made of rope. And on the vigil of the male or female saint, we didn't eat dinner in the evening, fasting on bread and water both on their vigils and on the feasts of the Most Holy Madonna, and we kept up these devotions throughout the octave[2]—all this, however, with the consent of our father and mother, who sometimes yelled at us but still let us do it.

Because of my infirmity, I ate little, and almost never any meat, for I was unable to hold food in my stomach, and I prayed the Most Holy Mother to bring me back to the condition of an ordinary person so that I could perform my housework better and suffer for the love of God. Having made this request to the Most Holy Mother, I heard an internal voice that told me, "Cecilia, you're born to obey and to let the will of Lord God be done, but it's your responsibility to command my dear Son." These words made me very fearful.

---

ies, who were very familiar with the symptoms of "the ugly sickness," never used the word or the euphemism in reference to her trances.

2. The week following a feast day.

Since my mother confessed to a *pievano* in the *contrada* of Santa Marina, whose name I don't remember [Cesare Turana], she took me to him to confess when I was around seven, but rarely. When I became ill at that time, I asked him the favor of administering communion to me before I died, and he granted it, giving me communion in bed. And I think he was my first confessor, to whom I made eight or ten confessions. Then my mother took me to confess to the priest Pisani, confessor to the nuns of Santa Maria dei Miracoli, who from then on was my ordinary confessor, for it was my desire to become a nun in that convent. Until his death I always confessed to him, and he recommended that the nuns receive me. After that I didn't have a designated confessor; but where my mother went, I went too—but rarely, that is, once or twice a year.

Since my father was in trade, he kept many young men in the house,[3] one of whom, called Pietro, became delirious. And one night, while I was praying and commending him to the Lord, I seemed to see that he intended to throw himself off the upper porch of the house. Hence I commended him even more fervently to God, and I saw great temptation surrounding that soul, for it appeared to me that the Devil wanted to push him down. And I believed that this was an illusion of the Devil meant to distract me from prayer. But the next day, two hours after sunrise, Pietro threw himself off the porch into the middle of the street. A priest from Santa Marina came running and, seeing that his bones and his head were all broken and he couldn't administer confession, declared him dead and left him that way. I started to pray, begging grace from God for the salvation of that soul. I was called to dinner by my father and mother, and while I was on my way, I heard Pietro, who had been laid on a table in a little chapel in our house, moaning. They called the priest, who confessed and anointed him, and at the hour of one he died.[4] So I had this vision from the Lord—but it could be, however, that it was a temptation to pay heed to those things I've always abhorred. I've always held my actions suspect in the eyes of God, for I'm a sinner and have done evil, and the good, if there has been any, is derived from God.

In praying, I've had many battles with the Devil, who appeared to me visibly either in the form of a frightening animal or as an ugly man breathing fire from his mouth. He used to snatch the Office I was using[5] and beat me, either with clubs or with iron rods, leaving my midsection battered. He

---

3. As apprentices or journeymen.

4. The register of deaths in the parish of Santa Marina corroborates Ferrazzi's account of Pietro's death, which occurred on 31 March 1627.

5. Probably the Little Office of the Blessed Virgin or a larger book of hours containing it.

kept telling me that it would be better to consent to marriage than to lead the kind of life I was leading and that I should leave alone what was his because I would come to a bad end, like so many others who have believed that they were serving God and were mistaken, and that he'd make me touch it all with my hand, and that I really should experience the taste of flesh. And I would respond naively—for I didn't know what he meant, except that I didn't like eating meat, and if I'd been able to eat it, I wouldn't have disobeyed my father and mother, who tried to force me to eat it—that not even for him would I eat it.[6] And I'd do everything I could to get him away from me, and he'd disappear with a great noise and stench. At the time, aged thirteen or fourteen, I hadn't yet told my confessors about this.

When I was around fifteen, my father and mother pushed me toward marriage, but I never consented. I begged them to make me a nun in one of the strictest orders there was so that I'd be more separated from the world. After about nine months, I was at work decorating a chapel in our house, making various things with my own hands, including figures of male and female saints, and I asked that the Most Holy Mother deign to console me by having my mother conceive a baby girl. A few days later she discovered that she was pregnant, at an age when she thought she wouldn't have any more children, having already given birth to twenty-two, boys and girls, all of whom are dead.[7] And then she gave birth to a baby girl, who is my sister living at Santa Teresa. Now that they had this other daughter, they agreed to my becoming a nun as I desired. After my sister was weaned, I had complete charge of raising her. One day when she was about eight months old, she fell off a bed. When she turned black and appeared almost lifeless, I carried her before a Virgin painted in the Greek style[8] and prayed on my knees that She bring my sister back to life, and I saw the Virgin spread Her arms and give her a benediction, after which the baby immediately recovered, unharmed. I took her to her cradle and said nothing to anyone.

Then came the plague, from which everyone in the household (father,

6. Translation based on a conjectural reading of a difficult passage. Ferrazzi claims not to have known in her early adolescence that the word *carne* could mean "flesh" in the sexual sense as well as "meat." As she must have realized by the time she dictated her autobiography, the "it all" the Devil wants her to touch must include his penis.

7. My search of baptismal registers in the parishes of San Lio and Santa Marina has turned up ten children of Alvise Ferrazzi and Maddalena Polis born between July 1604 and April 1617, four of whom died in infancy or early childhood. Since the register of Santa Marina covering the years 1619–35 is missing, the births of Maria and perhaps other siblings of Cecilia cannot be traced.

8. Some Venetian artists specialized in producing inexpensive Byzantine-style paintings of the Virgin Mary for devotional use in private homes.

mother, brothers, and all the servants) died,[9] leaving me all alone with my sister, who must have been about three, and both of us had the plague, too. My sister was tended by Frenchmen, but I refused to be treated by anyone, and so I cured myself by putting herbs on my sores, one of them under my arm and the other on my breast.

When I was with my sister in the house of Signora Modesta Salandi at the Carmini (having survived many travails, as I've told the Holy Inquisition in the past few days), alone in my room, a dove appeared to me several times while I was praying to the Lord to give me a good female superior who would rule me in accordance with the will of God. To my great amazement and consolation, the dove delighted me by flying around me, alighting now on my shoulders, now on my head, and then hovering around my ears. And the Most Illustrious Signora Marietta Cappello, having come there to talk with me, took me to stay with her near the Carità and had me confessed by one of those fathers, Father Corner. When he wanted to know what kind of life I led, I told him among other things about this dove. And he told me that I must send it away by throwing holy water on it the next time it came. So I did, but it wouldn't go away, even when I spit in its face as the confessor ordered me to do. Then he told me that if it wouldn't leave, I should command it in the name of God and the Most Holy Virgin to go to him, as obedience dictated. And from what that confessor told me, the dove did go to him; he added that I should learn from this how much obedience pleased God. Into this incident I've put nothing of my own, not considering whether it was God or the Devil.[10]

When I was in the house of the said Signora Marietta Cappello, whose husband [Paolo Cappello] had contracted dysentery and was near death, she had to go to their villa[11] on business, so she left me alone to care for the sick man. She sent from the villa a basket containing some thrushes, which I showed him to cheer him up, and he ordered me to prepare one of them for his dinner. But because I was so busy, being alone in the house, I forgot

9. In the great bubonic plague epidemic of 1630–31, some 46,000 Venetians died—approximately 30 percent of the city's population. See Paolo Preto, "Peste e demografia," in Comune di Venezia, Assessorato alla Cultura, *Venezia e la peste, 1348–1797* (Venice: Marsilio, 1979), pp. 97–98. The death register of Santa Marina for this period confirms Ferrazzi's account of its impact on her family. Only two of her brothers, by then adults who probably resided outside the parish, are not listed there.

10. That is, she is trying to recount this incident without drawing theological conclusions about it.

11. Paolo Cappello's will indicates that the villa was at Pagnano, near Asolo, about 64 kilometers (38 miles) northwest of Venice.

to pluck and cook it. While I was feeding him, for he couldn't even put his hand to his mouth, he asked me whether the thrush was cooked, but so as not to disturb him, I didn't answer. But going into the kitchen, I knelt down in the middle of it, begging the Most Holy Mother's pardon for my negligence with tears running down my cheeks. And as I knelt there, he called me, asking whether the thrush was cooked. And I, not knowing what to say because I couldn't bear to tell him that it wasn't even plucked, told him, "Right away, sir." And at the entrance to the kitchen, I met a little boy, handsome and graceful, who held in his hand a skewer with a roast thrush—exactly what he had ordered. Taking the thrush from the boy, I immediately carried it to the sick man and put it in his mouth a little piece at a time. He ate it with the greatest pleasure, thanking the Lord because it was so good. And I considered myself unworthy of having received so great a favor from the Lord. When he had finished eating the thrush and I had taken care of him, I returned to the kitchen, to the same spot where I'd been given the thrush by the little boy, and kneeling down, I began to flagellate myself, thanking the Lord and praying that whether He Who was master had sent it to me or it was the Devil, that food not cause harm. And so the gentleman was immediately relieved and cured. A few days later he got out of bed, to the wonder and amazement of the doctors and his wife.

Once while I was rocking a baby girl, daughter of the said Signora Cappello's daughter, sitting on the floor near the door of the room with my foot outside the sill, the housekeeper came by. Not realizing that my foot was outside the door, she shut it on my ankle. I didn't feel the pain until after midnight because while I was rocking that baby I was in a trance,[12] praying and meditating on the purity of the Most Holy Virgin through the purity of that little girl. I was carried to bed by Signora Cappello herself, who on instructions from my confessor, Signor Father Alvise Zonati, always assisted me in all my troubles. And in the morning, while they were talking about summoning the barber to treat me, I found myself completely recovered, thanks to the prayer I had made after midnight, in which I begged the Lord to heal me so that I could pay obedience to my lady superior.

I couldn't take communion except when the confessor and Signora Cappello permitted it, even though my desire to receive His Most Holy Body was very great. And one day, standing at the fireplace to do some chore and thinking about the greatness of God, Who is concealed in the accidents of that consecrated Host, I fell headfirst into the fire. Signora Cappello, who happened by at that moment, discovered me there and, con-

12. Literally, "outside myself."

siderably upset, pulled me out, finding me without any injury at all from the fire.

One day, a work day, the same Signora Cappello had me go to church for Mass in an apron all covered with blood by the sausage makers who were making salami with her. At the door of the church, my confessor, Zonati, asked me brusquely what I was doing there and ordered me to go into the belltower to ring for the Mass. I obeyed, even though I didn't know where the belltower was or which was the right bell, since there were four ropes, and I found the tower without getting the wrong rope. And without reconciling me he gave me communion during Mass, as he had done many times before without reconciliation. After giving me communion, he had me go into the confessional and wanted to know what I felt about that humiliation Signora Cappello had inflicted by sending me to Mass in such a dirty apron. I replied that my pride required nothing other than mortifications, which were few in comparison to my faults, and that I prayed the Lord to send them to me in secret so that no one would know about them, and to protect me from these external things so that they would do no harm to my soul.

Concerning the Carmelite confessor Master Bonaventura, assigned to me by the priest Polacco, vicar of the nuns, beyond what I have already testified to the Holy Inquisition, I say now truthfully that I've never talked with him except in the confessions I made at his feet or else in times of illness when I was in bed, wounded all over my body from the Devil scratching me while fighting with me for entire nights—especially when I was praying for some particular soul or for sinners or the souls of the dead (asking the Lord whether some soul was in purgatory), or for my sinful self. I talked with him about everything that had happened to me, both with the Devil and when I went into a trance, not knowing where I was with my body, which occurred frequently, both in church and at home. While I was at work during a trance, I'd run the needle through my finger without feeling a thing. And many times, under pressure to finish and consign my work on time to the person to whom I owed it,[13] I'd find it finished without knowing that I'd done so. Nor have I omitted on any count [to follow] his orders in everything he commanded in confession, during which he required me for the sake of obedience to tell him everything that had happened to me, in spite of some resistance on my part to speak because of the shame I felt. Never, while I was in his hands, did I do anything of my own free will. Since I couldn't take any food on account of that serious illness I had, I begged

13. Ferrazzi hints that she was supporting herself at least in part by doing needlework.

him to let me go for a few days without food, but he wouldn't permit that unless the physicians agreed. And he told me that I should choose death over disobedience. He always spoke harshly and reprimanded me, especially when I lost consciousness or went into a trance, commanding that I make a great effort not to do so.

And wishing to obey, I was overcome by a mortal illness, during which the physicians despaired of me because I had even lost the power of speech. In that condition, in the absence of the confessor, who had gone to say Mass, the Most Holy Virgin appeared with five saints[14]—the Carmelites St. Angelo [of Jerusalem], St. Albert [degli Abbati], and St. Elias, along with St. Ignatius the Martyr, to all of whom I was devoted—and stood around my bed. And the Most Holy Mother called me, telling me that it was time not for death, but for greater life. She took my right hand and told me that She had come with the saints to whom I was devoted in order to console me, and that I should promise to do what She asked. Furthermore, She showed me Her dear Son, whom I saw several times during the same illness, all cut and beaten up.

What She sought was this: that I stay in the world in order to suffer greater travails (those I'd experienced were nothing in comparison to those I had yet to survive) and that I remain firm for the greater pleasure and glory of Her dear Son. And that I promise to make in Her hands[15] this vow that She required of me: that is, never to depart from obedience to my superiors, who would be assigned to me by the will of Her Son; to let myself be abused and harshly treated for the salvation of souls; to agree to found the convent of Santa Teresa here in Venice,[16] which would be of great efficacy for the sins and salvation of the Republic; to regard those saints assisting Her as witnesses of the truth; to observe the life of St. Teresa with all the travails she had in this world, for I would have as many as she and even some more; to don immediately her habit, for God would give me more and more help; to prepare myself for hell and all its followers being open before me until the end of my life; and to ratify in the hands of my confessor the vow I had already made in the hands of the Holy and Most Blessed Virgin, Who told me that this convent would become the treasury of Her male and female

14. Ferrazzi names only four.

15. That is, placing her hands between those of the Virgin, as in the feudal ceremony of fealty.

16. Around 1638 Ferrazzi tried to establish a convent of Discalced Carmelites in Venice. She looked for assistance to a daughter of her protector Andriana Cuccina, named Francesca, a Carmelite in Bologna. This effort was blocked by her arch-antagonist, Giorgio Polacco. Rome, Archivio generale dei Carmelitani Scalzi, Plut. 202a: Provincia Venetiarum, "Historia Provinciae, Historica narratio de rebus Provinciae Venetiarum."

servants, adding that there would also be a monastery here in Venice for Her male servants.[17] I replied to Her with a mixture of great fear and consolation that since this was God's and Her will, I was content to have a longer life in order to do the holy will, even though I was a poor, miserable, ignorant sinner who didn't know what I was saying. When this was over, they disappeared with a most melodious sound, singing the Te Deum Laudamus,[18] and I myself awoke singing, in good health.

When the confessor returned, he came to my bedside and told me that I should give thanks to the Lord that, dead as I had been, He had given me life for greater service to Him. I told the confessor what had happened with the company that had been with me, and about the vow that I had to ratify in his hands and the habit I must put on. He gathered what was needed to dress me. Coming to say Mass in the house, in which there was a chapel, he gave me communion and blessed the habit. I put it on (and always wore it under my clothes), and I ratified the vow in the confessor's hands. And later the priest Polacco made me take it off, and I through obedience removed it, nor has he ever allowed me to talk about it, and I have obeyed, never putting it on again.

After nine years of suffering following this occurrence, my sister decided to remove me from the house and obedience of Signora Marietta Cappello, by force if necessary, for she didn't want me to be subjected any longer to such abuse and torments, and she decided to put me in the house of Santa Teresa, on which construction had begun, even though, following the priest Polacco's order, I was not involved in that project. And in that place, where I stayed a little more than a year, I was under the obedience of my sister, which seemed to me like a contradiction of obedience since the priest Polacco had ordered me not to observe this vow and I have always been assiduous about doing the will of God and that of my superiors. And in agreement with my sister, I went to a house near San Lorenzo, along with two servants.

A daughter of a gentleman of Ca' Lion at San Lorenzo [Paolo Lion], eight or nine years old, wanted to come stay with me, and I was glad to take her on condition that she not see her relatives except on rare occasions, for I didn't want her going anywhere or anyone coming to my house. And I, enjoying my holy poverty, did not get discouraged but had great confidence

---

17. Translation based on a conjectural reading of a difficult passage.

18. This hymn of praise, dating from the early fifth century, is sung every Sunday at matins when the liturgy includes the Gloria, as well as on such occasions for celebration as the ordination of a priest, the consecration of a bishop, or a military victory.

in God, Who has always provided for me, nor did I have any burden other than being head of the household, when before I had always lived as a subject under obedience. I found that I had nothing but a barrel of wine containing about four *secchie*, which my sister had given me when I left. And since she asked for the barrel back, I had to put that small amount of wine into a bottle left by certain merchants who had been in that house. Poured into the bottle, it turned out to be cloudy, so the serving women didn't want to drink it. But God's providence was so great that not only did that little bit of wine become good in that bottle, it multiplied to such an extent that it lasted seven or eight months for me, the serving women, and that girl until God sent me more. And when I reported that to Father Alvise, my confessor, he commanded that in holy obedience I not go to see whether there was a little or a lot.

In this period I got the disease of the stone, which sent me to bed suffering gravely. And my confessor made me take in a girl from Burano who was going around begging, telling me to keep her until the governors voted her admission to Santi Giovanni e Paolo, and I obeyed him. I kept that girl, who was always ill, for about four years, and then she died in my house. After that I took in three other girls for the sake of charity (with my confessor's consent, however)—very poor girls, sisters orphaned by the deaths of both father and mother, who were going around Venice seeking alms, and they too died in my house (in exemplary deaths, by the way).

Four or five months after I'd taken in those girls, I took in the little daughter of a prostitute, brought to me by a woman from the house of Signora [Andriana] Foscarini, who lives at San Trovaso. That woman snatched this girl from her own mother so that she wouldn't be ruined.[19] After she'd been with me a month, her mother found out and came to see her, and I showed off the girl, well dressed and taken care of. The mother rejoiced, telling me that if I would convert her, too, she wouldn't lead a sinful life any more. She left and then came back to bring me gold (that is, bracelets, chains, and rings, along with quite a few doubloons), saying that she'd let me keep them if I'd let her daughter go home with her for two or three days, after which she herself would change her life. I wouldn't take anything nor give her the little girl, telling her that I had received no such order from my confessor, and she said that she was satisfied to have the girl stay and I should keep the gold and the money, all of which she gave me. Not wanting anything, I told her to keep it all for herself for her own maintenance.

19. That is, be forced into prostitution.

One day I took this girl, whose name was Orsetta, with me to Mass at San Severo, and during the adoration of the Host, she ran away without my noticing and stayed away for three days, from Fat Sunday to the first day of Lent. Those three days I wept continually, praying God and the Most Holy Mother to do me the favor of telling me where she was and promising to be good and change my life. The first day of Lent, I went to church at San Lorenzo, and as I was weeping there for the loss of this girl, a beautiful young woman came to me dressed in dark blue with a glowing veil on her head—seemingly a foreigner, and I really believed she was a foreigner. She asked me, "Cecilia, where is Orsetta?" I replied without thinking, "Madam, you tell me where Orsetta is, I don't know," and I began to cry very hard. And she responded, "Leave here immediately and go to Santa Maria Mater Domini into a street called Calle Sporca."[20] Right away I went to my confessor and said, "Sir, I'm going to find Orsetta," and he gave me communion immediately without even reconciling me and told me to go with the Lord's blessing. But in my great haste I didn't tell him about that woman who came to find me, since she had said that I must leave right away.

I got into a gondola and had myself taken to Calle Sporca, where I had one of my maids get off and ask some prostitutes there whether there was a girl named Orsetta around. Some of them said there was and asked who wanted her, and the maids told them that it was her mother. Hearing that, they denied that she was there. When the maids reported this, I got out of the gondola and asked those women to show me where she was, telling them that they were greatly offending God by hiding that girl. One of them replied, "Yesterday evening an old man called Calafao[21] took her away." I didn't lose heart—quite the contrary, for I had an internal inspiration that the girl was in one of those houses. And when I asked when that old man would be back, they said that he'd come an hour or two after dark. Telling them that I wouldn't leave until he arrived, I asked them to give me shelter at the door of the house.

At the stroke of nones the old man appeared, and although I was calm inside, on seeing him I spoke harshly to put fear into him so that he'd give me that girl, for they had told me that he was supposed to take her to a nobleman's house. The old fellow denied having her, telling me that she'd gone away, and I ran up the stairs of the house with him after me. I gave the door at the top of the stairs a great push, and when it opened, I found the

20. The name means "Dirty Street."

21. Calafao means "ship caulker," perhaps a nickname derived from the procurer's primary occupation.

girl Orsetta with her hair all curled and dressed very showily, and the old man had come to take her away. Right away I hugged her and with loving words exhorted her to come back with me. She screamed that she didn't want to. And I, seeing her in that state, called my boatmen. When they scared her by saying that they'd take her by force, she yielded and came voluntarily into the gondola. Realizing that I had no money to pay the gondoliers, I found by chance a half-scudo on the ground in that street near that door. I had one of my maids pick it up and used it to pay the boatmen. And I took that girl home, where I locked her into a room so that she wouldn't escape again.

Getting back into the same boat, I went to the Zitelle to see the Most Illustrious Signora Marietta Barocci, who still lives there as superior, and I begged her on my knees to deign to take in that girl. I sent her [Orsetta] to the governors of the house, she was voted on, and the next morning the governesses came to my house to see her, and they took her to the Zitelle, where she still is. And her mother, instead of changing her life as she'd promised me, let herself be taken by a Jew and an Armenian onto a ship, on which they all died, and all that gold, along with the other things she insisted on giving me, was turned over to the girl in the Zitelle.

When my illness continued with excruciating pains, the physicians consulted and concluded that it might be the stone, for which they prescribed remedies that did no good. During the day, in the house at San Lorenzo where I lived, while I was praying the Lord to liberate me, a little friar appeared before me dressed as a Discalced Carmelite with that little white mantle. And I heard others, whom I couldn't see, say, "Don't worry, for this is Blessed Francis of the Baby Jesus, who has come to console you." And he, for whom I had particular devotion, showed me a winding road, full of stones, down which he wanted me to walk. But since I couldn't make my way down the road with all its obstacles, he went ahead and broke up those stones with a little hatchet like the ones the Stradiots[22] carry, saying, "It's by this road we must go to receive martyrdom for the benefit of souls." And while he split those rocks and enabled me to walk, he turned his face toward mine and showed me a city like Babylon, where a great number of people were doing bad things: men running after girls, looking as if they wanted to tear them to pieces; some of the girls fleeing and others running into the arms of the men, who undressed them immodestly. They looked more like devils than human beings. In my enormous anxiety I couldn't help exclaiming, "O Father, what dangers I see!" And when I said that, he replied,

22. Cavalry from Greece and Albania in the service of the Venetian Republic.

"O daughter, this is the martyrdom God has prepared for you for the salvation of these souls. Don't be afraid, for you must fight in the midst of them with great suffering and humiliation, and you must even risk your life. Lord God and His dear Mother will defend and protect you, and on account of great poverty you'll find yourself in a sea of lions, but nothing will harm you." Then I was filled with a great deal of energy and desire to suffer in order to support and aid those souls with the strength I requested from the Lord, the male and female saints to whom I was devoted, and in particular St. Joseph—though I considered myself a miserable sinner, without any merit before His Divine Majesty.

And after this, those sharp pains grew more and more, so that I broke plates and glasses with my teeth when they gave me food and drink to relieve me and keep up my strength. Confessors, physicians, and barbers tied me to a prayer stool, on which I was seated where one puts one's knees, and then they held onto it as hard as they could because I was jumping around with loud cries on account of the great pain I was in—but the stone couldn't pass. My body was covered with the habit of the Virgin, from whom I requested the favor that if these pains weren't enough, She send me others, but that She make sure that my body was covered and my private parts protected so that the Enemy[23] couldn't get at them, and that I lose consciousness on account of the sharp pains from which I was suffering. When it pleased the Lord, the stone came out, after I'd suffered ten or twelve hours of torment, leaving lakes of blood on the ground (for it came out of my mouth, too), and because for half-hours and even hours I couldn't recover my strength, everyone—confessors, physicians, and other laypeople—gave me up for dead.

And for the next nine years, every six months or at least once a year, I passed this stone, and after having done so I felt immense consolation in my soul, along with sorrow because the suffering had stopped. And every time I put my affairs in order, preparing myself for a good death, giving all my instructions as if it were the last time and begging the pardon of all my little ones for the bad example I'd given them and asking them to commend me to the Lord so that He'd have mercy for my sins and for the time I'd frittered away. And my confessor was the *pievano* of San Giovanni di Rialto [Antonio Grandi], and when I called him for assistance or to commend my soul to him, he would come and speak to me brusquely, saying that the Devil was tempting me in order to tempt him, too, and then he would speak gently, exhorting me to suffer.

23. The Devil.

After nine years, more or less, the problem got worse, so that I could neither sit nor stand nor walk. And if I sent for the said signor *pievano*, he couldn't come because he had so many important things to do, so that without this comfort, I was afraid that I'd fall into some temptation because the Devil was inveigling me, or that I'd throw myself out the window or kill myself. But I turned to the male and female saints to whom I was devoted. This torment lasted for two whole weeks because I couldn't pass the stone. And one morning at dawn, the Saturday of the Most Holy Mother,[24] I fell backward down a flight of stairs, the women of the house ran after me, and while I was at the foot of the stairs, Saints Francis Xavier and Anthony of Padua appeared to me and I had a great burst of energy.

I got into a boat with my women and had myself taken to San Giovanni di Rialto, went into the church, and asked that my confessor be called and that he come quickly because I was close to death. He sent a message saying that he was confessing the altar boys and to be patient because he would come. And instead, while I was waiting at his confessional, he had himself vested to say Mass. Then I prayed the Lord to give me enough strength to withstand the pains and asserted that for the sake of obedience I'd willingly die. And at this point one of those young altar boys came to read me the Passion of Jesus Christ, and if ever my pain was great, it was then, although it abated when I listened to the Passion of Christ. And at the elevation of the Most Holy Host, I made an offering to the Lord that through the authority of His servant,[25] either my pain lessen or I die if He wished, for I remained completely and in everything in holy obedience to Him.

All of a sudden I fell backward and cast out a mass of stones that would have filled a soup bowl, with a great deal of blood. And the signor *pievano*, after he took communion, brought the Most Holy Sacrament to me and gave me communion without reconciling me. As soon as he finished Mass, he came to find me, and I told him that I'd been dead but had been revived with the Most Holy Sacrament, but that I was a complete wreck. He went into his house and called for some handkerchiefs to wipe up those stones and the blood on the floor. He had me taken home in a boat and ordered me in virtue of holy obedience to pray to the Lord to give me the strength to go home. And so I went, in good health, and I've never suffered from or passed stones again.

Another time, when I was in the aforementioned church on St. Catherine's day,[26] that signor *pievano* called me into the confessional, but I didn't

24. Which of the many Marian feast days Ferrazzi is referring to here cannot be determined.
25. The priest celebrating Mass.
26. 25 November.

hear him right away because I had gone into a trance. And he, angry, started yelling at me in the presence of other people, saying "Wretch, is this the place to go into ecstasy? Get out of this church!" And he threw me bodily out of the confessional, and I left the church. I begged the Most Holy Mother to deign to remove these ecstasies from me, at least in public, so that I could obey my confessor, but all that happened was that the Enemy ceased to bother me by tempting me not to go back there, for I had been ordered not to return. But since I felt great sweetness and mental calm in my soul, I couldn't help going back there three days later, even though the people in church were saying that I had committed some great sin. When I came back, I begged his pardon, and he refused to pardon me but began with harsh words to drive me away. And before I left, I threw myself at the feet of a crucifix, begging it to help me, for I had been abandoned by my confessor. I heard a voice inside that told me, "Go, and leave everything to me. Obey blindly." So I went home, showing no sign of being disturbed. After two days the confessor came to my house at noon—I was at San Giovanni Evangelista—and summoned the doorkeeper to call me and open the confessional. I came, and he told me that he'd come to turn over the keys of the confessional because he no longer wished to confess either me or the girls. I replied that he was right, for ungrateful and proud as I was, I deserved worse, but I begged him to confess me one more time so that I could beg God's pardon and his. After several refusals, he said that he'd decided to do violence to himself, and he confessed me. While he was confessing me, I admitted my fault: that the only thing I was sorry about was the scandal I'd caused in that church. He replied that he realized the error he had made by yelling at me and calling me "wretch," but not to worry because he would restore my honor. He gave me absolution with tender affection and charity, confessed the girls, and continued for more than a year to confess us.

But when he was named confessor of the nuns of San Lorenzo, he sent me a message telling me that I should go to a Jesuit father named Chiaramonte and tell him everything he wanted to know, and so I did. First this father asked me how I had gathered those girls; then, so that he could govern my soul, he interrogated me about [my previous] confessor's method. Then he said, "Daughter, if you remain with that confessor, he'll drive you crazy." I went back to the *pievano*, who commanded me by holy obedience to tell him everything Chiaramonte had told me and what I'd replied. And the *pievano* gave me new instructions: that I go back to Chiaramonte to obtain absolution; that if [the Jesuit] questioned me on other matters, I should inform him; and that if he had ordered me to do certain things and Chiaramonte prohibited them, I should obey Chiaramonte. In confession, the signor *pievano* ordered me to take off the rings I usually wore, and when I went to Chiaramonte and he saw me without rings, he asked me why I wasn't wearing them. I told him that the signor *pievano*, my confessor, had ordered me in obedience to take them off. He retorted, "Why in the world did he let you wear them for nine whole years and now doesn't want you to wear them?" Very fearful, I went back to the signor *pievano* and told him this. He replied that I should do what [Chiaramonte] ordered, and for the next three or four months I went first to one of them, then to the other. Then the *pievano* told me that he had sent me to Chiaramonte to talk to him, not so that [Chiaramonte] would remove or abduct me from himself. Having heard what the *pievano* said, Chiaramonte ordered me not to go back but always to come to him for confession, as I did until another [Jesuit] father came—I don't recall whether it was Casati or Father Rodengo—after Chiaramonte was made provincial.

I remember now that after the plague, before I was put into Signora Cuccina's house, I was placed by order of Signor Molin in the house of Signor Antonio Maffei, who is still living. And I stayed with one of his sisters, Ippolita, a *dimessa*, who welcomed me very affectionately, and we were together for about a month and a half when she died. A week earlier, however, I'd foreseen her death. Because she flattered me and hugged me and praised to the skies everything I did, one night I got up out of bed very quietly so that she wouldn't hear me, for she always wanted me with her at night, and I began to pray, saying the Rosary of the Most Holy Mother and begging Her to free me from that woman's flattery. The Most Holy Mother of the Rosary, extremely beautiful, appeared before me and said, "Cecilia, don't worry that your purity will be compromised because this woman who is keeping you will very shortly be taken out of this world, so pray for her." The Most Blessed Virgin disappeared, leaving me very much consoled. Two hours after I had this vision, that woman woke up, weeping and fearful, and called me, looking for me in bed, but I was kneeling on the ground behind the curtain of the bed praying for her. I told her I was there and asked what she wanted. And she said, "Alas, what strange news! We must leave each other." I replied, "If it's God's will, we must have patience. We're born to die and go to enjoy Lord God." And thus, attacked by a light fever, she died within four days.

I remained alone in the house except for the maid because her brother was away from Venice. And since there was another brother in Venice who went out at night, I had to wait up to open the door when he came home and knocked at five, seven, or nine hours after dusk. But many times the Devil, not he, came to knock at the door. And going downstairs to open the door, assuming that it was he, I met the Most Holy Mother, a beautiful creature, Who told me, "Daughter, don't go open the door because you're mistaken. Go back to your prayers." And I immediately returned to prayer and heard the Devil yelling and beating at the door, making a great deal of noise. And this ruse of the Devil occurred four or five times. It made me very much afraid, but since I trusted in the Virgin Mary and my guardian angel, the fear passed.

Then Signor Antonio Maffei and his wife, who are both still living, came to Venice. And they had a little boy about five years old, a mute. In the morning when I dressed him and in the evening when I undressed him, I taught him prayers and asked God's grace that, if it were good for his soul, He deign to give him speech, and I prayed also that the Most Holy Mother do me this favor and not deny it to me. And I felt a great inner confidence that I'd receive it, as in fact I did, for he began to speak, to the astonishment and delight of his father and mother. He became a friar, I believe of San Giorgio, and he is still living.

Many times the Most Holy Mother appeared to tell me that I must distribute to [adult] sinners, boys, and girls the insignia of the Passion of Jesus Christ,[27] Who died for sinners. And with the consent and obedience of all the confessors I had at that time, three years before the plague, I had printed and made from wood, wax, and brass many [images of] Christ, which I gave away whenever the opportunity arose so that people would wear them—through which I've seen marvelous consequences of conversion and piety.

While I was in the Cappuccine [of San Girolamo], the priest Polacco ordered that I refrain from prayer, not say other prayers or do pious exercises that they [the nuns] wanted to do, and not even take communion. All I did was sleep on bare boards, as they did. But when I was in my cell while they were taking communion, St. Philip Neri, to whom I was particularly devoted, came vested for Mass to bring me the Most Holy communion. And when he put the sacred Host to my mouth, I didn't want to take it, nor did I, in order to fulfill the precept of holy obedience, for Polacco had ordered, as I've said, that I not take communion. That happened to me three times, and when the saint disappeared, I was left greatly consoled.

After leaving the *pinzochere* of San Martino, I was placed at the priest Polacco's order in the house of a gentlewoman at San Barnaba. And while I

27. Prints or medals representing the instruments of the Passion: the cross, the nails, the placard reading "Jesus of Nazareth King of the Jews," the crown of thorns, the sponge, the straw, and the lance.

was in a room praying for the souls of the dead, having gone into a trance, the Mother Vicar of the Cappuccine appeared before me sitting on a marble chair with a great flame resembling the mouth of a furnace in front of her. Seizing hold of my garment, she said, "Pray for me because I'm in great difficulty." I replied, "How can this be, Mother?" She answered, "Because of negligence in governing my novices." Then she took me by her hand, which was frozen, so that for two weeks my hand remained cold. I promised never to cease praying for her and ordering Masses until she was liberated. And shortly thereafter, word came to me that she was dead, which I hadn't known anything about.

After I'd been tormented for years by the stone, as I said before, as if gangrene had developed in those parts [of my body], Signor Dr. Michelangelo [Rota], who was a great friend and thought of me as a sister, consulted with Dr. [Francesco] Donadoni about injecting various oils into me with a syringe.[28] But when I refused, not wanting anyone to see me or touch my body, he asked my confessor, Father Alvise Zonati, to order me to do it. And when the confessor ordered it, I begged him not to command this, and he told me that God didn't want me to let myself contract gangrene. And Dr. Michelangelo having come in person to inject those oils with the syringe in the presence of the women, I begged him to be kind enough to wait until I'd asked the Lord. He left and returned the next morning to see whether I'd decided to let myself be treated. And I had my confessor summoned and recounted truthfully the following vision: that is, while I was praying about my difficulty, I saw at my bedside the Most Holy Mother with Her baby in Her arms, Who told me, "Cecilia, tell your confessor to refrain from making you obey this order, and to examine his cases of conscience,[29] for one can even die in order to avoid losing one's purity and one's virginity at the same time, and this is my dear Son's preference." She disappeared immediately, leaving me much consoled.

Having heard this, the confessor told Signor Michelangelo [Rota] not to do anything else. He [Rota] came to see me and found me entirely reassured. And I promised him that if he were to die before me, I would ask the Lord's favor to suffer for his sins and mitigate them with prayers and holy sacraments during the time the Lord made him worthy of suffering the pains of purgatory, and he promised to do the same for me if I died before he did. Signor Michelangelo died recently while I was in Padua in a state of great suffering and affliction, for the Devil was frequently beating me with chains.

28. That is, to administer an enema.
29. Theological manuals for confessors that explain how to handle particular instances of sin.

I learned from my confessor, who was the Jesuit Father Alessandro Zampi, that Signor Dr. Michelangelo had died. After several months during which I was praying for his soul, I saw a very beautiful and luminous young man carrying a limpid crystal vase in the form of a heart, as big as a *bozza* and full of the clearest water. Over its mouth was a golden ribbon and above that a flame of fire. He told me that he had appeared to me on God's behalf so that I would accompany him, and he led me along a very beautiful and charming road, and then he took me into another one so dark that it seemed like night, but the vase emitted such a glow that it was sufficient to light it. And he said to me, "Do you see this heart? Our conscience must be as clear as this water, this gold be the purity of our heart, and this fire be the great love we must have, persevering until the end of our life in order to receive this greater glory you'll see." Once he had said this, the road ended, and a great door swung open, behind which was Signor Dr. Michelangelo in an enormous fire carrying flowers. And then I saw a large table full of roses and fruits, surrounded by all my people—father, mother, siblings—and spirits who were singing and praising the Lord with the greatest thanks. Signor Michelangelo said, "O Cecilia, if I could come back to life, if the Lord allowed me to do so in order to improve my conduct, I'd be glad to leave Glory itself." While he was saying this, I very joyfully asked, "What do these flowers and fruits signify?" The young man replied, "These are the fruits of his good works, the flowers testimony to his virginity." Then he disappeared, and I thanked the Lord with the greatest satisfaction, telling Him that I, a sinner, was not worthy of this.

While I was living in Cannaregio, I was overcome by a most cruel illness with such atrocious pains all around my waist that I felt all the bones in my midsection breaking and a very hot fire burning within, so that I cried aloud day and night, which lasted for forty days. The physicians Michelangelo, [Pietro] Caffi, [Nicolò] Alberizzi, Donadoni, and [Pietro] Caimo attended me and prescribed various remedies that tormented me without providing any relief. Signor Caffi told the other physicians that they were all crazy because it was an infirmity sent by God, not a natural malady. They paid many visits, during which they told me I was going to die. Finally, on their last visit, they concluded that I couldn't last more than an hour, and therefore the signor *pievano* of San Geremia [Giovanni Conti], the *pievano* of San Giovanni di Rialto [Antonio Grandi], and Father Zuanne the Slav [Giovanni Andreis], confessor of the girls, came to me. The Most Blessed Virgin appeared at my bedside and told me, "Get out of this bed and go to the Sovereign Physician," showing me a large crucifix on the wall across from my bed. Right away—alone in the room while the priests, physicians, and noblemen were walking about on the porch weeping—I jumped out of bed with the great energy given me not by my nature, which in fact was destitute, but by Blessed God, and I put my mouth on His side, from which I sucked a water so precious that it spread throughout my body, cooling everything, and I was entirely free of illness.

And while I was praying that He give me the strength to support such great torments, I heard inside myself a voice that said, "Cecilia, I delight in this suffering of yours, but it is my will that you will feel these pains for three more days." And so it happened, for at midnight the same pains seized me again and lasted for three whole days. The physicians and priests who saw me attached to the crucifix and so rapidly restored to health were amazed, and a servant who was assisting me named Marietta [Elisabetta Bonardi][30]—now a nun of St. Teresa with Sister Eufrasia her superior in Conegliano—came to put a mantle over me while I was attached to the crucifix, and then she called in those on the porch mentioned above, who saw me healthy when before I had been all twisted and pale. They all rejoiced with me, but I told them not to celebrate so much because I had to suffer three more days, as happened.

Before the plague came, my sister who is still living, then called Maria, put a needle shaped like a fishhook into her mouth and swallowed it, holding it in her stomach for a whole week and feeling great pain. Many remedies, including holding her upside down, were tried, but none of them worked. At last turning to prayer, I prayed to God for my sister, who was in danger of dying. And I heard an internal voice that told me to take some lasagna noodles with a few greens and cook them in a pan with a little butter. That's what I did, my sister ate it right away, and two hours later she evacuated the needle, which was stuck in her intestine. I pulled out the needle, but because [part of] the intestine was outside and bleeding heavily, they summoned the barber, who touched the intestine with a hot piece of iron, and she was safe and sound.

At San Lorenzo I was keeping a girl whose name doesn't come to mind—she's alive, however, and is a lay sister in Santa Caterina [Chiara Poli]—and took another, a decayed gentlewoman from the Morosini family called Giulia, both of them very poor, who escaped from the house one morning at dawn. The night before they fled, as I was praying, an internal voice told me, "Watch out, Cecilia, you are about to suffer a great tribulation, but be prepared to follow the will of God, for you will be relieved." A

---

30. When the transcript of her dictated autobiography was read back to her, Ferrazzi corrected this name.

very beautiful young woman appeared before me and said that I must prepare myself because what I had heard during prayer was about to occur.

That morning, half an hour after sunrise, a girl came to me and said, "Signora, Giulia isn't here." And then a little later she told me, "That other one is missing, too." I was much afflicted by the loss of two virgins, who in addition had stolen some things, that is, gold and silver. Because they had no money of their own, they gave some of the silver to the boatman who took them to Fusina, and the rest they pawned at the loan bank of Padua.

I commended their virginity to the Most Holy Mother in order that She maintain them intact until I found them. I heard an internal voice that said, "Go toward Padua and you'll find them," and this I reported to my confessor, Father Alvise, so that he'd let me go. He didn't want me to, saying that they were in Venice and I'd find them, but I wept and told him that they were on the road, and so it was, for I saw them in my mind's eye. A gentleman came to see me, for in an office at the Palazzo Ducale he had encountered a boatman who turned in a silver fork and spoon that he said he'd received from two pretty, well-dressed girls who appeared to have escaped from a convent. The officials took the silver, and the nobleman, Sebastiano Barbarigo, brought me the boatman, who told me what had happened and said that they were waiting at Fusina for one of their uncles to come and take them away.

Immediately after obtaining my confessor's permission, I got into a boat with an old woman and went to Fusina to find them. At Fusina I rented a carriage, in which I went around looking for them. Everywhere I went, people told me that they'd seen them going by, and I had myself taken to the bridge at Noventa. After the bridge, their trail went cold. The next morning Father Alvise, my confessor, and the aforementioned noble came after me and found me on the other side of the Noventa bridge in the house of a friend of the woman who was with me. But since we couldn't find the girls, we returned to Dolo, where someone dressed as a pilgrim appeared—I don't know whether he was St. Anthony of Padua, whom I continually invoked—and asked me why I was so downcast and almost lifeless. My woman replied that I was going in search of two girls and couldn't find them. "I," said the pilgrim, "am here to find them." I took him right into the carriage, and we returned to the Noventa bridge. Arriving at an inn where there was a steward's wife, we asked her whether there were two girls there, which she adamantly denied. The pilgrim who had shown us that place disappeared the moment we got out of the carriage.

I went into the courtyard and saw the slippers belonging to one of these girls, as well as a handkerchief with lace edging which they'd taken from me, and from this I realized that they were there. After many requests and threats to the steward's wife, as well as giving her money, which she took, she still wouldn't admit that she had them. Finally, seeing the door of a granary, I said, "They're in here," and she retorted that it held her employer's grain. But on opening the door, I found one girl hidden under the haystack and the other behind a big canvas bag. They promptly begged my pardon, and I accepted them lovingly, led them to the boat, and took them home, where one stayed with me two more years and the other a year and a half.

One day I was at the house of Signora Marietta Cappello, who had removed me from the convent of Santa Teresa, where I was living; I remained with her for three days because she was resentful.[31] Her brother, Giovanni Morosini, had also come to stay with her. The evening before my departure, he engaged me in a conversation about the miracles of the Most Holy Mother that lasted two and a half hours. Hearing him discuss spiritual things greatly amazed Signora Marietta and her husband, for by no stretch of the imagination was that his habit. The next day I went back to the convent and commended him day and night to the Lord and the Most Holy Mother, intending to offer his soul to His Divine Majesty, as I did, so that He would give the man grace to change his life.

During the night, while I was making this request, my room filled with devils in the visible form of horrible animals breathing fire, who beat me, but I also saw the Most Holy Mother and the saints to whom I was devoted, who defended me. But the devils said that I shouldn't interfere with that soul, which was already theirs, or they'd take my life. With great confidence and living faith in the Most Holy Mother giving me strength, I prayed even more fervently. The devils disappeared, leaving me with bruises, pains, and a thirst so great that it lasted until daybreak. In a weak voice, I summoned one Madonna Chiara, who was in the convent, to bring me water to drink because I was unable [to get it myself]. Shortly the Devil in the form of this woman came into the room holding a little bucket, which she gave me, and when, before drinking, I said, "Jesus Mary," the Devil ran away, yelling and screaming so noisily that it seemed as if there were four or five carriages in the dormitory. The water only got as far as my lips, for the little bucket broke in my hands, and my head and lips swelled as if they'd been burned by fire. I knelt right down in the middle of the cell, thanking God and His Most Holy Mother and commending that soul even more strongly to God with the offer to suffer for his sins. And in the morning the news reached me that two hours after sunrise the noble, who'd been perfectly healthy,

31. Cappello was jealous of Maria Ferrazzi, who was trying to keep her sister at Santa Teresa.

had died suddenly. For this reason Signora Marietta sent someone to summon me, but I couldn't go because I was all battered by the Devil. The next day I went with great faith to San Nicolò, where I made my confession to the *pievano* [Giovanni Araneo] and took Communion, and as soon as I'd received the Most Holy Communion, I was completely free of all ills.

When I first went to stay with Signora Marietta Cappello, she decided to take me to Padua to the house of the deceased just mentioned [her brother], and while we were there, she summoned two of those fathers of St. Philip Neri, one named Father [Antonio Maria Corsino de'] Santi and the other Father Giovanni Battista Polacco from Feltre, who is still alive. She talked with them about me and what had happened to me; the fathers said they wanted to test me with a mortification. Signora Marietta had me called into the room where these fathers and her husband were, and the fathers asked me whether I was the one Signora Marietta had told them about. And they had two prayer stools put one on top of the other under the fireplace in that room. They told me to spit on my hands and ordered me to climb up on the prayer stools, get my hands thoroughly covered with soot, and then rub it all over my face. Without a second thought, I obeyed. Once I'd gotten down off the prayer stools, completely black, they took the chain of the fireplace, put it around me, and commanded me to go into the salon and pay my respects to some gentlewomen who were there. I did so. But as I was on my way, I saw near those ladies a foreign woman covered with jewels holding a baby by the hand, who beckoned me to pay my respects to her. I went to them, curtsied to them all, and left. On the way back I staggered a bit because of the chain, but a footman helped me. No one but that footman saw me—not the gentlewomen to whom I curtsied, for they told Signora Marietta that they hadn't seen me at all, although they certainly would have if I'd been there.

After all the trouble I had in Padua, I obligated myself to do all the good I could, especially to the poor, for the grace I'd received from St. Anthony when I called on him to let me find those two virgins. And when people came to me to ask that I take in girls, I took them willingly for the love of God without any compensation, and they have made themselves virtuous, having learned the way of the divine precepts.

The priest Polacco decided to put me in the convent of Santa Maria Maggiore and had me escorted there by three of the principal gentlewomen of the city, but those nuns all ran to the door of the convent, screaming that they didn't want me. When they persisted in their refusal and proved unwilling to yield to Polacco's persuasion and orders, he started shouting at them, saying, "I'm putting in a saint, one who lives on communion, one who has the stigmata!" Since they wouldn't obey, he told the nuns, "Unveil the Abbess [Maria Caterina], remove her from office!" but the nuns still wouldn't obey. Finally he began throwing some little slips of paper into the convent and told them, "I'm excommunicating you!" and the nuns threw them out, saying that they wouldn't accept his excommunication and that he had no authority to excommunicate them. And so we all returned home.

That night, while I was praying for that Mother Abbess on account of the improper names Polacco had called her, like "hussy," "rash," "insolent," and similar terms, I commended myself to the Most Holy Mother and heard a voice inside me that said, "Cecilia, obey blindly, because that's the will of your Spouse, and you must go get new crosses to bear that will be useful to those nuns' souls. Don't you aim at the salvation of souls? Don't bother about Polacco's having been offended when those gentlewomen hurt him by saying, 'You old madman, go learn how to dust your books!' and other inappropriate things, for this happened with God's permission. There wouldn't have been martyrs if there hadn't been tyrants. Go now, and carry on bravely. Let all your affection be for your Spouse and not for others."

The next day I was taken to the convent again by Polacco, Father Stella of the Frari, and those three gentlewomen. Patriarch Corner had written telling the nuns to obey because he knew whom he was putting in. Going inside the door, I knelt on the ground and kissed the Mother Abbess's feet. As I went in, Father Stella told me not to uncover my face or let those nuns see me until they'd escorted me to my room. Because of that order, Polacco had words with Father Stella, telling him that he mustn't interfere with me by giving me orders. When I was inside, the nuns said and did many injurious things to me, but when they got to know me, the Mother Abbess and all her nuns frequently caressed me and desired to spend time with me, although Polacco forbade them to seek me out. But when I prayed and asked God to remove the many signs of affection those nuns were showing me, twice the Most Holy Mother appeared to me, saying that although my purity and modesty were not at risk, I should still resist those caresses.

One day while I was there, Father [Giovanni Francesco] Priuli of the Somaschi came to the parlor, had the Abbess summoned, and told her abruptly to have me brought to him right away, for the Devil had made him come there. That's what the Abbess told me. I was led down; it was early in the morning on the day before Christmas, and I was in bad shape from the blows the Devil had inflicted on me that night. Without even saying good morning, he began, "Possessed one, bewitched one, the Devil brings you here! Did he bear the expense of your coming from so far away?" Then he told me to raise my head, asking me what I was feeling inside. I replied that although I wasn't worthy of that insult, I deserved worse for my sins. He added that I had nothing better to do than come from the Devil, that I was playing the holy woman to fool the world and waste poor clerics' time with ecstasies and apparitions. And he began to repeat, "Possessed one!" and stopped. Then he said, "Come on, I'll help you, and don't doubt God's goodness, and I promise to go to Vicar Polacco and come here every feast day." He left and went to Polacco and told him everything he'd done, asking that he be allowed to supervise me. But Polacco gave him a sharp reprimand, telling him that he was brainless and only wanted to take me away from him and that he himself hadn't given any such order.

It has come back to me that when Signora Marietta Cappello first took me into her house, she took me a number of times to the Giudecca to the Discalced Carmelite fathers, who then had a hospice there,[32] and she had me talk with Father Ferdinando, who came to the church of Sant'Eufemia and asked me to tell him everything that was happening to me. After he had examined me many times, Signora Marietta called him to the house, and that father, seeing a little gold chain with thirty-three links[33] on my right arm, yanked it off. And I thought my heart had broken, with such great pain that I fell to the ground in a faint. The father never returned that chain, saying in Signora Marietta Cappello's presence that he had discovered the Devil and that I was possessed. After the father left, I gave myself to fervent prayer, in which the Virgin appeared and told me, "Cecilia, don't be disturbed because this isn't the Devil, but you felt such pain when that chain was removed because you've made yourself the slave of Christ's Passion. Don't you remember when I gave it to you? A great outpouring of love produces gold and fire." I was left in great stillness, without any temptation, thanking God for having lifted that torment, and I felt so strong that I would have suffered any ill.

This gold chain was given to me in the following way. One day, under the obedience of Father Master Bonaventura the Carmelite, while I was in prayer at the hour of prime,[34] St. Bernardino of Siena, to whom I was particularly devoted, appeared to me with a basket in his hand that looked like gold, in which there was a gold packet of the mysteries of the Passion of Christ, but sprinkled with blood, and in the presence of the Most Blessed Virgin he put it in my hands. And I clutched it to my breast with great

---

32. By 1664 the Discalced Carmelites had moved to a new house, Santa Maria di Gerusalemme (next to the present railroad station), in which they still reside.

33. The number thirty-three symbolizes Jesus Christ's years on earth.

34. At 6 A.M.

tenderness, thanking His Divine Majesty that those instruments had been the salvation of the entire human race. And at the same time, the Most Holy Mother pulled that chain out of the basket and put it on my heart, but I wasn't aware of having it.

The next morning I went to the confessional and told the father confessor what had happened. He told me to touch my chest, and putting my hands on it under the veil, I felt that chain. And he, shouting, said, "These are temptations of the Devil! Go pray to the Most Holy Mother of the Carmine to remove these external things from you." While I was praying to the Most Holy Mother in obedience to my confessor, I heard internally, "You do well to follow holy obedience and pray for the souls of the dead so that they will be your advocates and witnesses of the truth." I took communion that morning and found that I didn't have the chain any longer. After communion I went back to the confessional, and the father inquired whether I had obeyed. I said yes, even though I was a sinner. I prayed to the souls in purgatory that whatever I could not obtain, they would supply, with this promise, that all the good I could do for those souls [I would do], that I would make myself the slave of their suffering, requesting a little of the pain of their punishments. And nothing else happened then.

One night before I went to the aforesaid Discalced Carmelite [Father Ferdinando], while I was praying at the hour of matins,[35] the Enemy came to me visibly in the form of a woman, who brought me some oranges and apples,[36] telling me that I should take them. I told her that obedience didn't allow me to eat them and that since I was about to take communion, this was no time to eat. She became so angry that, having changed from a woman into the Devil, he began to give me a tongue-lashing, saying that my confessor was a devil who would make me lose my soul and body and that I should leave him, and that he himself would not depart unless I promised to do so. And he showed me a bundle of iron rods, saying, "This will be your torment, and you'll remain in my hands." I replied that he could do what God permitted,[37] that I would do neither more nor less, and that God was the master, not he. He began to beat me with an iron rod until I was breathless and bleeding. And the Mother of God collected the blood, and I begged her not to do so but to keep everything hidden so that Signora

35. In the middle of the night (in convents and monasteries, 3 A.M.).

36. In seventeenth-century Venice, where oranges were an exotic luxury item, this was no ordinary plate of fruit.

37. Here Ferrazzi echoes the orthodox, antidualist position on the Devil: he is not an independent force of evil but acts only with God's sanction.

Marietta Cappello wouldn't see it. She replied that these [drops of blood] would in time become so many blooming roses. In the Virgin's presence the Devil disappeared, and going back to prayer in such bad condition, I acknowledged that I received everything from the hands of Jesus Christ, from whom I requested the favor of feeling a tiny spark of His Passion.

After that, a mob of devils came and threw a chain over me, tied me up, and dragged me repeatedly around the room as far as the door. Hanging on the back of the door was a thick hemp cord, which the Devil tied so tightly around my neck that I felt myself suffocating, and my throat was all swollen and my face black. Hearing the loud noise, Signora Marietta Cappello and her husband jumped out of bed, came running, and found me in that condition. They untied me and laid me on the bed, practically dead. And since I had a whip in my hand,[38] because the cord wasn't enough for the Devil, he took the whip from me and added it to the cord, twisting them together. They sent for Signor Father Alvise, my confessor, who had me tell what had happened and gave me a quarter of an hour to commend myself to the Lord. During that quarter of an hour, I went into rapture, during which the Most Holy Mother appeared and brought me the previously mentioned chain and put it on my right arm, welded in such a way that it couldn't be removed without breaking it. It was then broken and taken by the aforesaid Discalced Carmelite, causing me a great deal of pain, as I've said.

One day when I was at table with the said Signora Marietta Cappello, unable to hold food in my stomach as usual, she had me get up from the table and ordered me to take a walk under the portico. Doing so and looking down from the window at the *fondamenta*, I observed passing along it a young priest with chestnut hair, who fixed his eyes on me. Sitting down on a chair and going into a trance, I saw him in shadows that inspired a combination of fear and pity. For the next three days all I did was pray to the Lord for him, whom I didn't know, and perform penitential exercises—in obedience, however, to my confessor, Father Alvise, who gave me communion three days in a row for this soul. When the three days had passed, the confessor asked me who this priest was, and since I didn't know, he ordered that I pray to the Most Holy Mother to give me information about this man who was causing me so much difficulty. After communion I heard an internal voice that told me, "This is Abbot [Zuanne] Moro, who finds himself in the shadows of damnation." Three times another voice repeated, "Cecilia, pray for him without ceasing, for he will be given Glory." I was so consoled

38. In order to flagellate herself.

that I was too joyful to know what I was doing. Having thanked God and the whole celestial court, I started walking out to go home, and the confessor made me come back. He went into the confessional, and I told him all this. He replied, "Pray to the Blessed Virgin that, if this is not a diabolical illusion, She deign to open the eyes of your soul so that you can look at it."

The next night, while I was trying to pray but being persecuted by the Devil, who prevented me from doing so with many insolent acts, including taking the rosary from my hands and breaking it, I propped myself against the wall on my knees with my arms spread out. I began by saying, "My Lord Jesus Christ, I offer You this soul for the merits of your Most Holy Passion, promising You firmly to change my life and submit to any difficulty, persecution, and torments whatsoever. And I challenge Satan and all his followers." I prayed also to the Most Holy Mother of the Carmine. I saw that Abbot die in such accord with God that it looked as though he were going to a great jubilee. His guardian angel was there, and far away the demons were all trembling. I also saw an opened mouth of fire, ten *braccia* long, which he passed through, and immediately the Most Holy Mother covered him with her mantle and carried him into glory. I heard such a great harmony of instruments and voices that it lasted all night in my soul, for I was crazy and in a trance. And the next morning came the news that the said Abbot had choked to death. I revealed all this to my confessor, and I believe that he told Signora Marietta, for she then asked me many questions about it.

Once, as I was getting out of a gondola to go see the signor *pievano* of San Giovanni di Rialto, my confessor, I met a large crucifix coming toward me. Entering the church and commending myself to the Most Holy Sacrament, I heard an internal voice that told me, "Cecilia, that cross you just encountered, which then disappeared, is going to become much larger." And I was shown another one full of precious gems and still another big one full of spines and stumps, and I was asked, "Which of these two do you want?" I raised my mind to the Lord, thinking it over, and gave myself completely to the Lord's will. And I said, "Lord, in this life, give me not the one with gems but the one with spines." The one with spines was presented to me internally and I embraced it, feeling the most ardent desire for suffering. I came out of the trance with great rejoicing and happiness and revealed everything to my confessor, who yelled at me, saying that these were all temptations. And after having dressed me down, he sent me to commend myself to the Most Holy Mother of the Pietà in that church, and I did so. The next morning, without reconciling me, he gave me communion, and afterward he made me go into the confessional and told me that I should not be ungrateful for the special favors done to me by His Divine Majesty, but that I should be faithful to the cross He had given me and to the promise I had made Him.[39]

While I was living at San Giovanni Evangelista, Falsetti, the Pope's treasurer, accompanied by his pregnant wife, came to stay in Venice at the Carmini next to Ca' Vendramin. She summoned me, begging me to intercede for her with the Lord so that she would deliver safely, and she promised that if she had a baby girl, she would immediately give her to me so that I could raise her in the fear of God and keep her with me, for she would be mine. The time came, and finding herself in extreme danger because she couldn't give birth, she had me called. Waiting there until she gave birth, although with very great difficulty, I heard an internal voice that told me to take out my little cross and surreptitiously touch that woman's body. Once I had done so, she gave birth successfully to a baby girl, whom she immediately gave to me after she had been baptized in the house lest she die, for she was all black. I took her home and kept her for three days without food because I didn't have a wet nurse; all I gave her was a bit of cooked apple moistened with sweet almond oil. Once I'd found a wet nurse, I offered the little girl to the Most Holy Mother with great faith, and she proceeded to grow, intelligent and healthy.

After I had kept her for eighteen months, her parents decided that they wanted her back because the wet nurse, tempted by the Devil, was behaving badly. Before I gave her back, the Most Holy Mother told me that I shouldn't worry because even though I didn't have her, She Herself would exercise particular protection over her, and that her father wouldn't have her nor her mother, because they would not enjoy her [long], and that I should thank God that my efforts would be [rewarded] in heaven. After a few months they decided to take her to Rome. She died on the way, and having nowhere to bury her because they were at sea, they threw her into the water. She has appeared to me several times as an angel in heaven, reciting the Hail Mary and sometimes the Magnificat.[40] While I was praying, she strolled around, very beautiful. Assuming that it was some kind of illusion, I made the sign of the cross and threw holy water at her, but she didn't go away.

Signora Marietta Cappello married off one of her daughters, who had a baby girl, and since they couldn't find anyone to nurse her, for all [the wet

---

39. Translation based on a conjectural reading of a difficult passage: the word translated here as "promise" is marred by a scribal error.

40. The Virgin's hymn from Luke 1:46–55, frequently sung at matins and vespers.

nurses] had lost their milk, they gave her to me when she must have been eight or nine months old. I took her and, commending her to the Lord, made her some pap with holy water. The little girl ate and slept well, and so I kept on giving her the same food. With her left leg twisted in such a way that the foot was turned to the left side and the calf of the leg came around in front, she was bereft of human aid, for none of the many remedies that were tried did any good. On the morning of Corpus Domini[41] when she was around two or three years old, after I had commended her to God at vespers, I was called by Signora Marietta and left the little girl sitting on a chair. She got up by herself and began to run around the room, to the surprise and delight of everyone in the house.

One day while I was going to Mass at San Giovanni di Rialto, I ran into a nobleman, who asked me for alms.[42] I told him that I had no money, as in fact I didn't. Immediately I heard an internal voice saying, "That's not how your father behaved." And it crossed my mind that for many years a noble came to our house at night to ask for alms, and my father brought them to him secretly; he even got out of bed at midnight to do so. Then I was told, "Look into your purse," and sticking my hand in, I found many silver coins. Turning back, I gave all of them to that nobleman. I went into church to confess, telling the *pievano*, my confessor, what had just happened. He dressed me down, saying that the Devil was leading me astray and I shouldn't have given [the man] those coins. Then he had me recount the incident again, and when I had done so, he said that I had done right, but that another time I shouldn't give the man the coins without showing them to him first. And he sent me to the feet of a [picture of] St. Catherine the Martyr,[43] telling me to stay there with my face on the ground for two Misereres[44] because I had given that money outside of obedience. The Most Holy Mother with St. Catherine appeared to me there, and they ordered me to ask my confessor's pardon and give him the message from them that charity brooked no delay. So I did.

One day while I was praying near a window overlooking the tiled roof of the church of San Severo, in through it came a young nobleman with long hair, dressed in red silk garments, who intended to assault me. Immediately I was called by the Most Holy Mother, Who said, "Cecilia, beware of

41. A movable feast celebrated in mid- to late June.
42. Not all Venetians of noble rank were rich.
43. Probably Domenico Tintoretto's *St. Catherine with Angels*.
44. The time needed to recite the penitential Psalm 51, *Miserere me Deus* ("Lord, have mercy upon me")—in this instance, twice.

that dragon, that rapacious wolf, who seeks to devour the virgin's blood." And the young man pleaded for his life, begging me to let him leave the house quietly. And having escorted him, with the Virgin's help, down the stairs, which he descended on his knees without my seeing his face, I opened the door for him, and he took my skirt and kissed it, crying for pardon and mercy. This fellow went to confess to Signor Father Alvise, told him what he had done, and became good, leaving the woman he was keeping. The confessor told Signora Marietta this. Going back upstairs, I thanked the Most Holy Mother for the favor She had done me.

While I was living in Cannaregio, I was assaulted by a most cruel illness, beyond the one I've already mentioned, for which I commended my soul [to God]. And Father Chiaramonte, who was my confessor, came to my bedside to assist me and stayed with me all night. He noticed, I don't know how, that I had on a chain as thick as a finger and a half with links the length of half a finger attached in the back and fastened with a padlock. He asked whether I would remove it if he commanded me to do so for holy obedience. I asked him to give me a little time because I could not take it off except with great pain. He had recourse to prayer, and on returning he told me that he was giving me three days to take it off. Not knowing what to do, not wanting others to lay their hands on me and not being able to do it myself because of the extreme pain I felt, for it had grown into the skin, I called on the Glorious Virgin Mary, went into a trance, and three days later found myself with the chain detached from my flesh without any pain at all. When the father confessor came, I gave him the chain with the greatest embarrassment and shame, for I had never allowed anyone to know about it, and truly I don't know what he did with it, having paid no attention because I was much preoccupied by illness.

That chain was given me by a hermitess who lived at Santa Marina across from my house when my parents were still alive and I was about eight years old, and I took pleasure in watching her, peeking at her very often through a hole in our upper porch, through which I saw her in her room, which was in the attic of the house of a gold-leaf maker, and I often heard the angels sing in the greatest harmony. One morning when I was with my mother at Mass in the church of Santa Marina, so was this hermitess, who took communion every day and died in the odor of sanctity.[45] Leaving my mother, I went to her side, commending myself to her with great submission and embarrassment so that she would pray to the Lord for me, who was so

---

45. That is, with the reputation of having been a living saint and possibly a candidate for beatification.

bad and disobedient to my mother, and telling her that it was my most ardent desire to serve God. She welcomed me with great tenderness and told me, "Daughter, don't worry, for I've been observing your soul for a long time, and look what I've brought you." And she showed me the chain, saying, "This is what will keep you mortified and will give you grace to obey your father and mother, but it will prick you, and therefore bear this torment for the Passion of Our Lord. Before you put it on, go to the *pievano*, your confessor, [to see] whether he is willing to give you license [to wear it]." (She had already shown him the chain.) The *pievano* granted his permission but first gave me communion. Thus, I went home and, without saying anything to my father and mother, put it on, and I always wore it until Father Chiaramonte noticed it. After it was taken off me, I don't know by whom or how, as I've said above, many ulcers remained on my flesh. Signor Dr. Caffi prescribed remedies to heal them, but all in vain. Later, one night I woke up with those sores healed.

The hermitess moved house at the order of that signor *pievano*, and no one knew where she was. About four years after she had given me the chain, when I was in prayer one day and went into a trance, she appeared to me in agony and said, "Cecilia, I'm leaving you. Now is the time to pray for me because I'm going to render account to God for my good and bad deeds." I returned to consciousness, and that evening, another trance having come upon me, I saw that blessed soul go to heaven, accompanied by huge crowds of angels and saints with a most beautiful melody. The next day, while I was working beside my mother, I went into a trance, and she gave me a kick in the side. I quickly jumped to my feet and rushed to lean out a little window, through which I was deemed worthy to see her corpse being carried to burial accompanied by an enormous crowd of people.

After a year had passed, while I was in prayer, the aforementioned hermitess appeared to me with her skirt full of flowers and fruits to tell me that she was praying for me and that these were the fruits and flowers of my deeds and sufferings. The hermitess disappeared, leaving behind her an intense aroma that lasted for many days.

I have always been particularly devoted to St. Catherine the Martyr, who many years ago, a week before her feast day, gave me a very beautiful ring inset with thirty-three diamonds, one more lovely than the other. While I was in rapture, she put it on the little finger of my right hand.[46] I saw it, but not everyone else did. One day when I was in church at San Giovanni di Rialto, it was seen by a girl who was there, and she pointed it

46. In this vision Catherine of Alexandria permits Ferrazzi to replicate her own mystical marriage.

out to a few other girls. Noticing this, I fled blushing into the confessional and told everything to the signor *pievano*, who retorted brusquely that I didn't choose to conform to the will of God and preferred to repeat what was being said in church.[47] I left the confessional all upset and with the intention of not returning home, and I went to my sister at Santa Teresa. I stayed there all day in the choir and returned home at the Ave Maria.[48] One day, in confession at San Severo with Signor Father Alvise, having the ring on my hand, I showed it to him. He told me that I should make a promise to God that when obedience demanded, wherever I might be, I would give it to Him. During communion, when I was in rapture and he [Father Alvise] was celebrating Mass, He ordered me to present the ring to the celebrant. I'm in no position to know whether I gave it to him. It's true, however, that I saw it on the altar near the chalice on top of the corporal,[49] and the whole altar shone. When I had come out of rapture, he called me into the confessional and asked whether I had obeyed. I replied that I had, and he added that I should thank God that obedience had been executed. And so I did. That ring had remained on my finger for a week before and a week after the feast.

Since some proclaimed that I was a saint and others that I was possessed, the priest Polacco decided to have me exorcised. The first exorcism, from which he removed me saying that [the exorcist] didn't know his business and was afraid of spirits, took place at the Cappuccine. The second was at San Martino at the house of the Dominican Tertiaries in a little courtyard. He was present, though a bit removed, and he ordered a certain priest named Domenico, a man of great fame, to put the stole on me. In attendance as well were a friar from San Giobbe, one from Santo Stefano, and one from the Frari,[50] all of whom stood around me and exorcised me, and I was sitting on the knees of the friar from San Giobbe, and all of them whispered in my ear that God give me patience and exhorted me to suffer willingly for the love of God. After this exorcism, which lasted an hour and a half, they decided that I should kneel at Polacco's feet, kiss his hand, and tell him, "Sir, this spirit of mine wants Most Holy Communion every day to deliver me from this torment." He gave me the benediction, saying, "The Lord bless you, I understand everything." During the exorcisms I felt the

---

47. Translation based on a conjectural reading of a difficult passage. Apparently Grandi was rebuking Ferrazzi for using the confessional encounter to report what others were saying, rather than concentrating on her own sins.

48. Around 6 P.M.

49. The cloth on which the priest places first the chalice, then the host.

50. Identified in the first interrogation, above.

greatest consolation and throughout, I saw the Most Holy Virgin nearby, for it seemed to me that I was in paradise.

When I was at San Lorenzo, alone in my room, someone appeared to me dressed in black in a Jesuit habit, though I didn't know who these fathers were because there were none of them in Venice.[51] Appearing beside my bed, he began to console me, exhorting me to suffer those pains mixed with contempt for myself, which would be a liquor exceedingly efficacious for purifying my soul, and he told me that until the end of my life I'd have to suffer these mortifications, which would continue to grow. A girl, still alive, whose name doesn't come to mind (she was related to a servant at Ca' Canal), entered my room, and seeing that Jesuit, she ran upstairs to tell the other girls that I was doing evil with a gentleman. And hearing this, I rejoiced and prayed to the Most Holy Mother to reveal to me who this person was. She appeared and told me that it was Ignatius [Loyola], Her adopted son, whom She had sent me for my consolation, and that I shouldn't worry because he wouldn't be seen. And thus I was consoled.

In the confessional at San Giovanni Evangelista with the signor *pievano* of [San Giovanni di] Rialto, who was reprimanding me as usual, I told him, "Sir, let me leave, because a great tribulation is about to occur," but he wouldn't allow me to depart. Though I asked him three times to let me go, he said that I must stay there for obedience. And while I was with him, a great fire broke out below ground and burned the entire section of the house where the oven was without burning the bread, which was outside in baskets and also in the oven. The girls went forward, and the signor *pievano* began to distribute communion, but seeing the fire, which was spreading, he began to tremble with the pyx[52] in his hand and wanted to leave. I told him fervently that he should remain firm and have faith in the Most Holy Sacrament, for this was a temptation of the Devil. Communion proceeded without the fire harming anyone because it stayed within bounds until the service was over. When I'd put all the girls in a room and the said signor *pievano* had gone out of the house, I had him come and give a benediction to that fire, which having been blessed, went out immediately. Meanwhile a crowd had gathered.

I recall that when I was in the Cappuccine [of San Girolamo], I took a pair of scissors to cut off my hair, for I desired to put on the habit and stay

51. Expelled from Venice in 1606 during the confrontation between the government of the Republic and Pope Paul V known as the Interdict Crisis, the Jesuits were officially readmitted in 1656.

52. A round box with a hinged lid that holds the large host used in the benediction section of the Mass.

with them. And when I was about to start cutting, the Most Holy Virgin appeared and took the scissors from my hands, saying, "Is this the express obedience you promised Me?" I bowed, asking her pardon and telling her that I'd be content to stay there not as a nun but as a slave if that pleased Her. She repeated the aforesaid words and disappeared.

One time when I was taken to Murano by Signora Marietta Cappello, she took me to the Capuchin mothers, who were busy with the conservation of their church.[53] Seeing me, the Abbess [Maria Benedetta Rossi] persuaded me to go into the convent, telling me that she'd leave the door open so that I could flee inside, but first she'd draw Signora Marietta aside so that she wouldn't notice or try to stop me. Agreeing readily, I went through the door, but as I passed through it I was held from behind. Turning to see who was holding me, I saw that it was the Most Holy Mother, Who said, "Is this obedience to your superior?" and disappeared. I went right to Signora Marietta, revealed my error, and was much relieved. The Abbess called me, complaining that I hadn't fulfilled my promise, and I told her that such was the will of God.

While I was with the said Signora Marietta at San Severo, in prayer around midnight, I heard internally [someone] telling me to commend the soul of a religious who was about to pass from this life. I prayed to the Most Holy Mother that Father Alvise wake up and go help that soul, if this were the real voice of God. The third time I prayed, the priest who was called to help the soul awoke. Not knowing who had called him or where he was supposed to go, he went out of his house and knocked on the door of Ca' Benzon. Told that no one there needed anything and that they didn't like having their door knocked on at that hour, he was at last sent downstairs to see whether an abbot staying there or any of his servants, who had all been fine that day, needed anything. They found the abbot dying. Hence, Father Alvise confessed him and gave him extreme unction, and he died immediately. After that prayer I was assailed by the fiercest of illnesses, during which I heard an internal voice telling me, "Cecilia, suffer, for these sufferings of yours will save that soul." And I was completely consoled.

This is what I want to reveal to the judicial authorities in order to obey, although with very great embarrassment, for I've always tried to hide everything, holding myself to be a great sinner, as in fact I am, with no merit before His Divine Majesty, and considering myself unworthy even of being on this earth. And whether the aforementioned things I've deposed were illusions of the demon, as I've always suspected and feared, I leave to the

---

53. Ferrazzi, or her scribe, mistakes islands. The "Capuchin" convent of Santa Maria delle Grazie, recently established at the time of her visit, was on Burano.

appropriate people to judge, submitting entirely and forever to their will and judgment. At the urging of the Most Illustrious Monsignor Patriarch, while I was on my deathbed at Sant'Antonio I made my last will, leaving what little I had to be distributed to the girls, except those who chose to leave without either becoming nuns or marrying.[54] I had no money, nor do I have any at present, but rather debts, as one can understand, since unfortunately I've had to spend for the girls, trusting only in God, Who provided as necessary in ways that stunned and amazed me. And if I've left anything out through a lapse of memory, for I'm in bed with a continual fever, I protest that I never want to transgress against the obedience I have always desired to pay to all my superiors. I have governed my girls in accordance with the rules or constitutions I wrote with the approval of the Jesuit Fathers Zampi and Casati, which they thought over very carefully, as one can see.[55]

At the order of the Most Reverend Father Inquisitor General in the entire Most Serene Domain of the Venetians, the aforesaid Cecilia dictated all this to me, Friar Antonio da Venezia, Reader in Sacred Theology and Consultant to the Holy Office, which, read to and, as she affirmed, well understood by her, she confirmed and signed with her own hand.

[signed] I Ceilia Ferraci[56] confirm.

Friar Antonio da Venezia, as above, deputy.

[Tuesday,] 15 July 1664. In the presence of the Most Excellent Lord Procurator Morosini. Before the Most Illustrious and Most Reverend Lord Apostolic Nuncio and the Most Reverend Father Inquisitor General and the Vicar of the Most Reverend Lord Patriarch of the Venetians, the aforementioned Reverend Father Friar Antonio da Venezia, deputy as above etc., presented the above, written by him and dictated to him by the aforementioned Cecilia Ferrazzi, swearing and touching etc. [to confirm that] he had faithfully written down everything she had dictated.

[signed] Andrea Vescovi, Chancellor, etc.

54. In this will, written on 1 July 1661 but never probated, Ferrazzi also left some clothing and furniture to her sister and requested burial in the church of the Gesuiti, provided that the Patriarch agreed. VeAS, Notarile, Testamenti, busta 65 bis (Andrea Bronzini), no. 250.

55. A copy of regulations for her house, in which it is given the name Seminary of the Immaculate Conception of the Virgin Mary, is inserted in the Trial Record.

56. Again, notice Ferrazzi's vacillation in the spelling of her name.

APPENDIX 1
PERSONS MENTIONED IN THE TEXT

Letters and numbers in parentheses indicate locations on the map of Venice, pp. xxx–xxxi.

Alberici, Nicolò (b. c. 1627)   Physician, native of Bergamo. He testified during the defense phase of Ferrazzi's trial on 27 January 1665.

Alberto degli Abbati, St. (d. 1307)   Sicilian Carmelite saint, canonized in 1475. His name was frequently invoked for assistance in exorcisms.

Aldrovandi, Giovanni Battista, S.J. (1609–67)   Jesuit, Venetian provincial of his order from 1663 to 1664. Ferrazzi uncharacteristically mangles his surname. On 6 April 1665, at the central headquarters of the Holy Office in Rome, he responded to questions framed by the defense. Like the testimony furnished by his fellow Jesuits, Aldrovandi's was decidedly favorable to Ferrazzi.

Altoviti, Iacopo (1604–93)   Native of Florence, papal nuncio in Venice from 1658 to 1666. The abbreviation *etc.* alludes to his benefice, the archbishopric of Athens, a see in Ottoman territory often assigned to high-ranking curial bureaucrats.

Andreis, Giovanni (c. 1615–1683)   Born in Trau (Trogir) on the Dalmation coast; staff member at the church of San Marcuola (I-5) and confessor to its hermitesses there. He testified on 24 July and 12 August 1664, during the prosecutorial phase of Ferrazzi's trial, and again on 27 January 1665, during the defense phase. Named bishop of Lesina (Hvar) in 1667, he was transferred to the see of Trau in 1676.

Angelo of Jerusalem, St. (1185–1225)   Carmelite martyr who met his death at the hands of a Sicilian heretic; canonized in the fifteenth century.

Anthony of Padua, St. (c. 1190/95–1231)   Friar of Portuguese origin, joined first the Augustinian order and then the Franciscan. He was famous as a preacher, healer, and exorcist.

Antonio da Venezia, O.F.M.Obs.   Identified as Ferrazzi's scribe in these documents. Nothing further is known about him. A board of consultants with credentials in theology, of which he was a member, provided advice on thorny points when the Holy Office requested it.

Araneo, Giovanni (d. 1648)   *Pievano* of San Nicolò (C-14) from 1623. He expired after having been bitten by a rabid dog.

Barbarigo, Sebastiano q. Zuan Alvise (1594–1662)   One of Ferrazzi's two main patrician supporters. He lived near the Carmini in the parish of Angelo Raffaele (E-13), not far from Santa Teresa (C-13), the convent founded by Maria Ferrazzi, which may explain how he and Cecilia met.

Barbaro, Isabella Zen   Widow of Alberto Barbaro and stepmother of Zorzi Barbaro. For three months in the early 1660s she managed the house at Sant'Antonio di Castello (X-13) while Ferrazzi was in Padua for medical treatment. Although her name was on the list of witnesses submitted by the defense, she was not summoned to testify.

Barbaro, Zorzi q. Alberto (1633–99)   Listed among the witnesses for the defense. He was never called to testify.

Barocci (Barozzi?), Marietta   Unidentified. Almost no records of the Zitelle (N-17) for the seventeenth century survive.

Bartoli, Daniele, S.J. (1608–85)   A major literary figure in the Jesuit order. He was questioned in Rome, along with his colleagues Aldrovandi and Rodengo, on 6 April 1665.

Bernardino of Siena, St. (1380–1444)   Famous Franciscan preacher, canonized in 1450.

Bonardi, Elisabetta di Francesco   Known while she was in Ferrazzi's care as "Betta marangona" (Betsy the carpenter's daughter). She was interrogated on 4 August 1664 at the grate in the parlor of the convent of Santa Teresa in Conegliano.

Boselli, Alessandro, S.J. (1587–1660)   Named head of the Venetian Province of the Jesuit order in 1650, several years before the Jesuits were officially readmitted to Venice (see *Autobiography,* note 51).

Caffi, Pietro q. Fausto (c. 1581–1677)   One of the physicians who treated Ferrazzi. He testified on 12 August 1664 and 22 January 1665.

Caimo, Pietro (b. c. 1609)   Physician. In 1661 he had testified in an investigation conducted by the Provveditori sopra Monasteri of a disturbance at Ferrazzi's establishment at Sant'Antonio di Castello. He was called to the stand as a witness for the defense on 22 January 1665.

Cappello, Cecilia Daughter of Marietta and Paolo Cappello, married Francesco di Filippo Querini on 30 April 1640. She was probably younger than Ferrazzi. Her father's will, written in 1662, mentions two daughters of Cecilia and Filippo Querini, Mariettina and Lauretta, one of whom may be the baby mentioned by Ferrazzi. VeAS, Notarile, Testamenti, busta 187 (Pietro Antonio Bozini), no. 495.

Cappello, Marietta Morosini (c. 1594–1676) Patrician who hosted Ferrazzi in two palazzi belonging to the family of her husband, Paolo Cappello (one in the *contrada* of Santa Giustina [Q-8], the other near the church of San Giovanni Laterano [P-8] in the *contrada* of San Severo). Questioned on 25 August 1664 and again on 23 March 1665, Cappello denied or professed not to remember most of what Ferrazzi claimed occurred during her stay with the Cappello family.

Cappello, Paolo q. Cristoforo (d. 1662) Husband of Marietta Morosini Cappello.

Casati, Paolo, S.J. (1617–1707) Important Jesuit confessor. Another of his confessands was Queen Christina of Sweden, whom he instructed in the Catholic faith in preparation for her conversion. In September 1668 he wrote to Ferrazzi expressing sympathy for her problems with the Inquisition.

Catherine of Alexandria, St. (d. 305) Martyr. According to legend, this royal convert to Christianity entered into a mystical marriage with Christ, more than held her own in theological discussions with learned men, and was tortured by being run over by a spiked wheel before being decapitated. She is the patron saint of maidens and many other social and occupational groups. Her iconographical attributes are a crown, a book, and a wheel.

Chiaramonte, Girolamo, S.J. (1600–1676) Head of the Venetian Province of the Jesuit order, 1656–59. For unknown reasons, he was not called to testify.

Conti, Giovanni (d. 1669) *Pievano* of San Girolamo (G-13) from 1654 until his death. He testified on 19 January 1665.

Cornacchioli, Giacinto (c. 1599–1673) Native of Ascoli Piceno (near the Adriatic coast in central Italy), and therefore in Venetian eyes a "foreigner." He gained some reputation as a musician before becoming a priest. At the time of the trial he was chaplain of Sant'Antonio di Castello. Interrogated on 8 August and 18 December 1664 about the recycling of Ferrazzi's portraits, he claimed to have functioned merely as a middleman who hired someone else to do the job; he was evasive and contradictory about that painter's identity.

Corner, Federico q. Zuanne (1579–1653)   Appointed cardinal by Pope Urban VIII in 1622 and patriarch of Venice in 1631. This influential and wealthy prelate retired to Rome in 1644. For his family chapel in the Roman church of Santa Maria della Vittoria he commissioned Gian Lorenzo Bernini's statue of St. Teresa in ecstasy.

Corner, Giacomo Antonio, O.S.B. (b. c. 1605)   Abbot of Santa Maria della Carità (I-13), a monastery belonging to the Lateran Canons but run by Benedictines. He confessed Ferrazzi at the suggestion of Marietta Cappello and testified for the defense on 19 May 1665.

Cuccina, Andriana (c. 1577–15 November 1647)   Member of a family, the Giavarina, who came originally from Bergamo, as did that of her husband, Francesco di Alvise Cuccina. (He is one of the children depicted in Veronese's *Presentation of the Cuccina Family to the Virgin.*) Having made a fortune as jewel merchants, the Cuccina family owned a palazzo on the Grand Canal, now Palazzo Papadopoli (near J-9). Six children were born to Andriana and Francesco between 1601 and 1616. One of them, Francesca (in religion, Maria Andriana di San Giovanni Battista), became a Discalced Carmelite nun at San Gabriele in Bologna.

Domenico (priest)   Famous exorcist called in by Polacco to treat Ferrazzi. Nothing further is known about him.

Donadoni, Francesco   Physician about whom no additional information is available.

Elias, St.   Old Testament prophet, who according to the Carmelites was the founder of their order.

Falsetti. *See* Farsetti

Farsetti, Antonfrancesco (1606–1676)   A wealthy Tuscan businessman who held various important financial posts in the papal administration under Urban VIII; purchased his family's way, first into the Roman nobility. and then, in 1664, into the Venetian patriciate. He and his wife, Eugenia Pavia, had eight children, three of them female. Since Placidia married and lived until 1693, the short-lived daughter they entrusted to Ferrazzi was either Teresa or Eugenia Maria.

Fasana, Caterina Contarini   Probably a patrician woman, about whom no further information is available.

Ferdinando, O.C.D. Discalced Carmelite who ripped the chain off Ferrazzi's arm. No further information about him is available.

Ferrazzi, Alvise q. Martin (c. 1582–1 December 1630)   Cecilia's father, a *casseler* (maker of wooden boxes and chests). His daughter seems to have been correct about his having roots in Bassano.

Ferrazzi, Maddalena Polis (c. 1580–26 December 1630)   Cecilia's mother, probably a native of Venice.

Ferrazzi, Maria (1623–88)   The only one of Cecilia's many siblings to survive the plague of 1630, founder of the Calced (Ancient Observance) Carmelite convent of Santa Teresa. Through extraordinary entrepreneurial efforts she built the convent into a flourishing house. She established other convents in Verona, Padua, and Vicenza. Her name in religion was Maria Angela Ventura of the Most Holy Sacrament.

Foscarini, Andriana q. Lazzaro Mocenigo (d. 1668)   Patrician who married Zuan Battista q. Sebastiano Foscarini in 1628. In a will drafted on 29 September 1662 she left sixty women's shirts to "those girls who are at Sant'Antonio di Castello under the governance of signora Cecilia," provided that the establishment was still in operation at the time of her death. VeAS, Notarile, Testamenti, busta 1267 (Agostino Zon), no. 39. On 23 March 1665 she testified in Ferrazzi's defense.

Francis of the Baby Jesus, Blessed (1544–1605)   Francisco Pascual Sánchez, Spanish Discalced Carmelite, whose accomplishments included saving the city of Valencia from the plague and founding a convent for repentant prostitutes.

Francis Xavier, St. (1506–52)   One of the original companions of Ignatius Loyola, who spearheaded the Jesuit missionary effort. Along with Ignatius, Philip Neri, and Teresa of Avila, he was canonized in 1622.

Giera, Bartolomeo   Doctor of laws and *pievano* of San Bartolomeo (M-9). He served as Patriarch Giovanni Francesco Morosini's vicar general.

Grandi, Antonio (d. 1662)   Canon of the ducal church of San Marco (O-11), *pievano* of San Giovanni di Rialto (L-8) from 1644 until his death.

Hermitess of Santa Marina   Unidentified.

Ignatius Loyola, St. (1491–1556)   Spanish founder of the Society of Jesus, canonized in 1622.

Ignatius of Antioch, St. (d. c. 107)   Martyr, bishop of Antioch. He is believed to have been fed to the lions in Rome.

Lion, Paolo q. Pietro (1612–80)   Patrician who helped Ferrazzi establish her first house (next to his own) and put two of his daughters in her care. He testified strongly in her favor on 28 March 1665.

Maffei, Antonio *Cittadino* who befriended Ferrazzi. (In her first reference to him, Ferrazzi mistakenly gives his first name as Francesco.) At the time he took in Cecilia, he was living in Sant'Aponal (K-9), the same neighborhood as her late uncle and aunt. He and his wife, Cristina, had five sons, born between 1620 and 1629. The one who miraculously recovered from muteness and became a canon of San Giorgio in Alga cannot be identified. By the time of the trial, Maffei had moved to another parish, was thought to be out of town on business, and therefore did not appear as a witness.

Maffei, Ippolita (c. 1585–1631) Pious woman whose death from a persistent fever occurred only twelve days after that of Ferrazzi's uncle and aunt. Cecilia may have been engaged to nurse her.

Maria Caterina, Abbess of Santa Maria Maggiore (D-11) Served two terms (1636–42) in this office. No other information about her is available.

Molin, Francesco q. Marino (1575–1655) Patrician who found lodging for Ferrazzi after the death of her uncle and aunt; elected doge in 1646.

Moro, Zuane q. Girolamo (b. 1621) "Abbot" of Santa Maria della Misericordia (K-5), a church to which the patrician Moro family had the right of appointment. The holder of the position was popularly but inaccurately titled abbot.

Morosini, Giovanni di Francesco (1588–1646) Marietta Morosini Cappello's eldest brother.

Morosini, Giovanni Francesco di Giovanni (1604–78) Patriarch (that is, archbishop) of Venice from 1644 until his death.

Morosini, Pietro q. Michiel (1598–1667) Elected procurator of San Marco (member of the board that managed the extensive property holdings of the ducal church throughout the city) in 1647. On 9 June 1660 and again on 11 March 1664 the Senate elected him *savio all'eresia.*

Philip Neri, St. (1515–95) Native of Florence who founded the Congregation of the Oratory; canonized in 1622.

Pinzoni, Bonaventura, O.Carm. (c. 1594–c. 1673) Friar who helped Maria Ferrazzi establish Calced Carmelite convents in Venice, Padua, Verona, and Vicenza. He testified on 12 August 1664 and again on 27 January 1665 during the defense phase of the trial.

Pisani (first name unknown) Confessor to the nuns of Santa Maria dei Miracoli (N-7), and Ferrazzi's confessor early in her life.

Polacco, Giorgio (1570–c. 1654) Venetian priest who for more than thirty years served as confessor to the Benedictine nuns of Santa Lucia (E-8). From 1631 to 1644 under Patriarch Federico Corner, and occasionally between 1647 and 1651 under Patriarch Giovanni Francesco Morosini, he held the post of vicar in charge of female religious. In several of his numerous published works he alluded to his experiences with Ferrazzi.

Polacco, Giovanni Battista   Oratorian priest who wrote numerous spiritual pamphlets published in Padua during the 1660s. One of them, a translated abridgment of a guide for nuns by St. Francis de Sales, was dedicated to Ferrazzi. On 8 September 1664 he was questioned about her by the inquisitor of Padua.

Poli, Chiara q. Antonio (in religion, Domenica)   Dominican nun who testified on 28 July 1664. She alleged that Ferrazzi had engaged in sexual relations with the steward of Ca' Lion and spoke of other irregularities at the house for "girls in danger" at San Lorenzo (Q-9).

Polis, Defendi (c. 1573–5 November 1631)   Cecilia's maternal uncle; like her father, an artisan.

Polis, Margherita (or Marietta) (d. 5 November 1631)   Defendi Polis's wife, hence Cecilia's aunt.

Priuli, Giovanni Francesco (in the world, Maffeo) q. Francesco (1596–1681). Head of the house of the Somaschi at Santa Maria della Salute (M-4) from 1651 to 1663.

Raimondo da Venezia, O.F.M.Rif.   Friar, almost certainly one of those who exorcised Ferrazzi. He had run afoul of the Venetian Inquisition in 1635 for promoting reverence for Luisa de Carrión, who was then on trial by the Holy Office in Valladolid for pretense of sanctity.

Renieri (daughters)   Probably Angelica and Clorinda. See Renieri, Nicolò.

Renieri, Nicolò (1591–1667)   Flemish artist who settled in Venice in 1626 and became the most famous portraitist of his era in the city. He trained his daughters Clorinda, Angelica, and Lucrezia as painters. (At the time of Ferrazzi's trial, Clorinda was married to the painter Pietro Vecchia and Lucrezia to the painter Daniel Vendich.) On 26 March 1665, when Renieri was questioned about his portrait of Ferrazzi, he confirmed that it had been altered by someone else to resemble St. Teresa.

Ricetti da Iseo, Clemente, O.P.   Inquisitor general of Venice from 1632 to 1639. He questioned Ferrazzi in 1637.

Rodengo, Camillo q. Aurelio, S.J. (c. 1610–80)   Prefect of the Jesuit college in Bologna at the time (14 February 1665) when he was questioned by the inquisitor of Bologna on articles submitted by Ferrazzi's defense team.

Rossi, Maria Benedetta (in the world, Elisabetta) (d. 1647) Under the religious name of Adriana, became a nun in Santa Maria del Redentore (Cappuccine di San Girolamo, L-18). In 1624 she and six other nuns founded Santa Maria delle Grazie on Burano. After the plague of 1630 she began negotiations for the establishment of a third convent, Santa Maria del Pianto (Le Servite, Q-7), completed after her death.

Rota, Michelangelo Physician about whom no additional information is available.

Salandi, Modesta q. Francesco (c. 1587–1678) Widow of Paolin Casoli. She hosted the Ferrazzi sisters for a certain period, probably in the late 1630s, in her home near the Carmini (F-13). Salandi stayed in close contact with Maria, who protected her in her old age, but not with Cecilia. Perhaps because of her advanced age, she was not called on to testify during this trial.

Santi, Antonio Maria Corsino de' Theatine priest (not an Oratorian, as Ferrazzi states), based in Padua.

Spinelli, Giovan Paolo Father of two daughters, Lucrezia and Cornelia, who had spent twelve years in Ferrazzi's care in all four of her houses and who testified for the defense on 17 March 1665.

Stella, Michiel, O.F.M. (c. 1577–1652) Friar who resided in the Conventual Franciscan house, Santa Maria Gloriosa dei Frari (H-10). Nothing more is known about him.

Stoppa da Venezia, Nicola, O.E.S.A. Augustinian friar, almost certainly one of those who exorcised Ferrazzi. He was brought to trial by the Venetian Inquisition in 1667 for sexual abuse and extortion connected with his practice of exorcism.

Stroiffi, Ermanno (1616–93) Artist who became a priest in 1647. He helped to introduce the Congregation of the Oratory, founded by St. Philip Neri, to Padua and Venice. Stroiffi was interrogated about his portrait of Ferrazzi on 27 January 1665.

Teresa of Avila, St. (1515–83) Founder of the Discalced Carmelite order for women; canonized in 1622. Her works, particularly her autobiography, were often cited by priests attempting to "discern the spirits" of visionary women.

Turana, Cesare *Pievano* of Santa Marina (M-8) from November 1583 until his death in November 1628; Ferrazzi's first confessor.

Ugoni, Agapito, O.P. (c. 1602–74) Member of a noble Brescian family who joined the Dominican order around 1627. After many years teaching philosophy and theology in Dominican houses of study, he was appointed inquisitor in Vicenza, where he served from August 1652 until January 1663. Promoted to the position of inquisitor general of Venice in February 1663, he held this post until his retirement in June 1670.

Valentine, St. Probably a conflation of two third-century martyrs. He specialized in curing convulsions and epilepsy.

Vendramin, Francesco q. Zuanne (c. 1599–1672) Key supporter of Ferrazzi who purchased the headquarters for her last establishment and testified vigorously in her behalf on 7 May 1665. In her will probated in July 1663, Vendramin's wife, Lucrezia Trevisan, left 1,000 ducats to provide a marital or monastic dowry for a girl she and her husband had placed in the house at Sant'Antonio di Castello, as well as a large bequest in cash and jewels to Ferrazzi. VeAS, Notarile, Testamenti, busta 1139 (Angelo Alessandri), no. 176.

Vescovi, Andrea (1622–1714) Chancellor of the Holy Office, 1654–1709. He succeeded his uncle, Antonio Vescovi, in the chancellor's position, which he left when he was elected *pievano* of Santa Maria del Giglio (Santa Maria Zobenigo, K-12). Among his writings, none of them published, is a list of Venetian holy people.

Zampi, Alessandro di Cesare, S.J. (1623–1702) Jesuit who, along with his colleague Rodengo, was questioned about Ferrazzi by the inquisitor of Bologna on 14 February 1665.

Zogalli (Iogalli), Giovanni Priest who served on the staff of the parish church of San Felice (K-6) and as confessor to the nuns of Santa Giustina (Q-8). He was nicknamed "the theologian" because unlike most Venetian priests he held a doctorate in theology.

Zonati, Alvise q. Francesco (c. 1600–1654) Chaplain of San Severo (P-9), spiritual director of Marietta Cappello and eventually of Ferrazzi. He also served as confessor to the nuns of Sant'Antonio di Torcello. In his will he left 100 ducats to Ferrazzi "so that she will pray to God for me." VeAS, Notarile, Testamenti, busta 152 (Francesco Beaciani), no. 116.

Zusto, Alvise q. Francesco (1609–65) Elected *savio all'eresia* in March 1664.

APPENDIX 2
PLACES MENTIONED IN THE TEXT

Letters and numbers in parentheses indicate locations on the map of Venice, pp. xxx–xxxi.

Bassano (del Grappa)   Town 77 kilometers (46 miles) northwest of Venice in the Venetian province of Vicenza.

Burano   Island in the Venetian Lagoon, site of Santa Maria delle Grazie. See Cappuccine di Burano.

Cannaregio   Northwestern *sestiere* of Venice; site of Ferrazzi's third house for "girls in danger," which may have been near the convent of the Cappuccine di San Girolamo.

Cappuccine di Burano   The convent of Santa Maria delle Grazie, founded in 1624 by Maria Benedetta Rossi and several other nuns from Santa Maria del Redentore in a former Servite monastery. Despite their nickname, the nuns followed the Servite Rule. Their church contained a miraculous image of the Virgin believed to have been painted by St. Luke, brought there from Constantinople in the mid-fifteenth century.

Cappuccine di San Girolamo (L-18)   The convent of Santa Maria del Redentore (called the Cappuccine although the nuns followed the Servite Rule), located in the northwestern part of Venice near the church of San Girolamo in the sestiere of Cannaregio. The convent was established in the late 1580s.

Carmine, Carmini   See Santa Maria del Carmine.

Castello   Easternmost *sestiere* of the city; see also Sant'Antonio di Castello.

Conegliano   Town 60 kilometers (36 miles) north of Venice.

Dolo   Small town 24 kilometers (14 miles) southwest of Venice, about halfway to Padua.

Este   Small town 71 kilometers (43 miles) southwest of Venice, near Monselice.

Frari   See Santa Maria Gloriosa dei Frari.

Fusina   Port on the mainland opposite Venice, from which boats went inland via canal and river.

Gesuiti (N-5)   Jesuit church, Santa Maria Assunta, located in the *sestiere* of Castello. Built in the twelfth century for the Crociferi, it was turned over to the Jesuits in 1656 when they were readmitted to Venice.

Giudecca   Island just south of the main part of Venice across the canal of the same name; administratively part of the *sestiere* of Dorsoduro.

Mirano   Hamlet 20 kilometers (12 miles) west of Venice, near which the Cuccina family had a villa.

Noventa   Spot 6 kilometers (4 miles) northeast of Padua on the road from Venice; site of a bridge across the Brenta River.

Padua   Important city under Venetian control, 40 kilometers (24 miles) southwest of Venice; site of a famous university, the basilica of Sant'Antonio di Padova, and a house for "girls in danger" run by Ferrazzi for two or three years before her arrest and trial.

San Barnaba (H-13)   Parish church not far from the Carmini.

San Fantin (L-12)   Parish church in the *sestiere* of San Marco, near which was the meeting place of the Confraternity of San Girolamo and Santa Maria della Giustizia, called the Company of San Fantin. Members of the Company performed the pious work of accompanying condemned criminals to their execution.

San Francesco della Vigna (R-8)   House of the Observant Franciscans, located in the northern part of Venice.

San Giovanni (Elemosinario) di Rialto (L-8)   Church on the south side of the Rialto bridge and market. It was under the jurisdiction of the ducal church of San Marco, whose canons appointed its priests.

San Giovanni Evangelista (H-9)   One of the four Scuole Grandi (prestigious confraternities) of Venice, across from which is the confraternity's church. Ferrazzi's second house for "girls in danger" adjoined the church; through a grate in the window, she and her charges could see and hear the celebration of the Mass without being observed.

San Lio (N–9)   Parish church in the western part of the *sestiere* of Castello, not far from Piazza San Marco.

San Lorenzo (Q-9)   Prestigious Benedictine convent, from which the surrounding neighborhood took its name, in the parish of San Severo; site of the first of four houses for "girls in danger" run by Ferrazzi, which was next door to Ca' Lion, the residence of her early patron Paolo Lion.

San Marcuola (I-5) Parish church in the *sestiere* of Cannaregio; three hermitesses lived there immured in its walls.

San Martin[o] (S-10) Parish church in the *sestiere* of Castello, near which was a house of Dominican *pizzochere*.

San Nicolò (C-14) Parish church in the *sestiere* of Dorsoduro.

San Severo (P-9) Parish church in the *sestiere* of Castello. Its four chaplains were appointed by the abbess of San Lorenzo.

Santa Caterina (L-5) Benedictine convent in the *sestiere* of Cannaregio near the Discalced Carmelite monastery, Santa Maria di Nazareth.

Santa Maria dei Miracoli (N-7) Franciscan convent in the eastern part of the *sestiere* of Cannaregio, not far from Ferrazzi's childhood home.

Santa Maria del Carmine (F-13) Church of the Calced (Ancient Observance) Carmelite order, which held a miraculous image of the Virgin and Child (the Madonna del Carmine). Nearby was a house of Carmelite *pizzochere*.

Santa Maria della Carità (I-13) Monastery of the Lateran Canons, in this period under the direction of a Benedictine. The monastery is now a museum, the Gallerie dell'Accademia.

Santa Maria Gloriosa dei Frari (H-10) Headquarters of the Conventual Franciscans, nicknamed by Venetians "the big house."

Santa Maria Maggiore (D-11) Originally a hermitage of *pizzochere* associated with the parish church of Sant'Agnese, which became a Benedictine convent in the late fifteenth century. Its church, modeled on the Roman basilica of the same name, contained a miraculous image of the Virgin. The church is still standing; the site of the convent is now occupied by a women's prison.

Santa Maria Mater Domini (G-7) Parish church in the *sestiere* of San Polo.

Santa Marina (M-8) Parish church in the *sestiere* of Castello, demolished in the nineteenth century.

Sant'Antonio (Abbate) di Castello (X-13) Monastery of the Canons Regular of San Salvatore, near the lagoon in the southeastern part of the city. In this neighborhood, a "charitable zone," were hostels for retired seamen and musicians, a home for pious widows, and other houses of refuge and treatment. Ferrazzi's fourth and last house was an enormous palazzo adjacent to the monastery. Owned for about a century by the Venetian state, which used it as a guesthouse and then rented it to the nobleman Domenico

q. Carlo Ruzzini, the palazzo was put on sale in 1658 to help finance the War of Candia, a long conflict between Venice and the Turks. Ferrazzi's supporter Francesco Vendramin (acting alone, not with Sebastiano Barbarigo as she suggests) spent 15,115 ducats to purchase it for her and her "girls." In 1668, after Ferrazzi's disgrace, he set up a boarding school for a limited number of poor noble girls, called Santa Maria della Concezione (Le Concette), under the supervision of a group of Capuchin nuns from Mantua headed by Lucia Ferrari. At Napoleon's order, this entire area was cleared in 1807 to establish the Public Gardens.

Sant'Aponal (K-9)   Parish church in the *sestiere* of San Polo.

Santa Teresa (C-13)   Calced (Ancient Observance) Carmelite convent founded by Maria Ferrazzi, Cecilia's sister, with the help of Bonaventura Pinzoni and financial aid from various Venetian patricians. Maria and her companions moved into this house, located in the parish of San Nicolò in the southwestern part of Venice, late in 1643.

Sant'Eufemia (H-17)   Parish church on the Giudecca.

Santi Giovanni e Paolo (O-7)   Large Conventual Dominican church in the *sestiere* of Castello. Near it was a refuge for poor girls founded in 1528 by pious layfolk in collaboration with priests of the Somaschi and Barnabite orders. Its official name was Santa Maria dei Derelitti, but Venetians called it the Ospedaletto (little hospital) (P–8). From 1566 on its more talented inmates were trained in music; hearing a concert there became an obligatory stop on the tourist itinerary. As Ferrazzi's account of the girl from Burano indicates, the boards of governors of this and similar institutions examined and voted on candidates for admission.

San Trovaso (H-14)   Parish church in the *sestiere* of Dorsoduro.

Zitelle (N-17)   House of refuge on the Giudecca for "girls in danger" established in 1559 by several patrician women with support from Barnabite and Jesuit priests. In the 1660s its population numbered around 250. Its male governors took charge of finances; female governors oversaw day-to-day operations and screened candidates for admission, from whom a substantial entry fee was demanded. Since by law the Zitelle was restricted to daughters of patricians and *cittadini*, placing Orsetta the prostitute's daughter there meant that Ferrazzi had to exert her considerable influence, no doubt enhanced by the money and jewelry turned over to her by the girl's mother.

GLOSSARY

bozza A liquid measure.

braccio (pl. *braccia*) Measurement of length, equivalent to about 60 centimeters (just under 24 inches).

Ca' (contraction of *casa*, followed by surname) The house of a patrician or wealthy citizen family. See also *palazzo*.

calle Venetian term for street.

cittadino A member of a small, legally defined category of Venetians who had the right of access to certain offices.

contrada Administrative district, named after and coterminous with a parish.

dimessa (pl. *dimesse*) A pious woman living a secluded life who devoted herself to teaching the catechism and to engaging in various charitable activities. Companies of *dimesse* were established in Venice and on the island of Murano in the late sixteenth century and elsewhere throughout northeastern Italy in the first half of the seventeenth. Although members of these groups originally intended to follow a "third way" (other than marriage or the convent) of serving God in the world, the institutional Church did its utmost to turn them into cloistered nuns.

doge The head of the Venetian Republic, elected for life by the Senate.

don Honorific title (from Latin *dominus*) applied occasionally to priests and always to Benedictine monks.

fondamenta Sidewalk running along the edge of a canal.

palazzo A large building, either a private home or an edifice housing government offices.

Palazzo Ducale   The residence of the Doge and headquarters of several branches of the Venetian government.

pievano   Chief priest of a parish church, a position of great prestige. Venetian *pievani* were elected by the membership of the parish council (well-heeled patricians and *cittadini*). Since almost all the seventy parish churches in Venice were served by more than one priest, *pievani* supervised a staff including other priests and clerics in lower ranks, such as acolytes and deacons.

pinzochera   (Venetian *pizzochera*, pl. *pinzochere*)   A pious unmarried or widowed woman, comparable to the Iberian *beata*, who made an informal promise (as opposed to a legally enforceable vow) to live in poverty and chastity, either in a group setting or in her own homes. Some *pinzochere* were loosely affiliated with a male monastic order. Until the late sixteenth century, becoming a *pinzochera* was a viable alternative to marriage or the convent for a devout woman—especially one unable to pay a marital or convent dowry—who wished to pursue the religious life in the world. Once the decrees of the Council of Trent began to be enforced, however, the life style of *pinzochere*, who were compelled to take formal vows and subjected to enclosure, came to resemble that of nuns.

q.   (abbreviation of the Latin *quondam*)   Son or daughter of the late (father's name follows). Given a relatively small pool of first names and the existence of large patrician clans with many branches, specifying the father's name was essential to establishing a person's identity.

secchia   (pl. *secchie*)   A wooden bucket used to collect milk.

sestiere   One of the six administrative districts of Venice, three of which—Cannaregio, San Marco, and Castello—lie north of the Grand Canal, while three others—Santa Croce, San Polo, and Dorsoduro—lie to the south.

signor, signora   Lord, lady; sir, madam. Terms of respectful address often omitted in English but almost invariably present in early modern and contemporary Italian usage.

BIBLIOGRAPHY

Secondary sources are grouped by subject under the following headings: The Misogynist Tradition, The Other Voice, Power and Obedience, Pretense, Purity and Danger, The Roman Inquisition and Venice, and Writing and Speaking. Some titles are listed under more than one subject heading.

PRIMARY WORKS

Alberti, Leon Battista (1404–72). *The Family in Renaissance Florence.* Trans. Renée Neu Watkins. Columbia: University of South Carolina Press, 1969. (Translation of book 3.)

Ariosto, Ludovico (1474–1533). *Orlando Furioso.* Trans. Barbara Reynolds. 2 vols. New York: Penguin Books, 1975, 1977.

Astell, Mary (1666–1731). *The First English Feminist: Reflections on Marriage and Other Writings.* Ed. and introd. Bridget Hill. New York: St. Martin's Press, 1986.

Barbaro, Francesco (1390–1454). *On Wifely Duties.* Trans. Benjamin Kohl. In *The Earthly Republic,* ed. Benjamin Kohl and R. G. Witt, pp. 179–228. Philadelphia: University of Pennsylvania Press, 1978. Translation of preface and book 2.

Boccaccio, Giovanni (1313–75). *Concerning Famous Women.* Trans. Guido A. Guarino. New Brunswick, N.J.: Rutgers University Press, 1963.

———. *Corbaccio or the Labyrinth of Love.* Trans. Anthony K. Cassell. 2d rev. ed. Binghamton, N.Y.: Medieval and Renaissance Texts and Studies, 1993.

Bruni, Leonardo (1370–1444). "On the Study of Literature (1405) to Lady Battista Malatesta of Montefeltro." In *The Humanism of Leonardo Bruni: Selected Texts,* trans. and introd. Gordon Griffiths, James Hankins, and David Thompson, pp. 240–51. Binghamton, N.Y.: Medieval and Renaissance Texts and Studies, 1987.

Castiglione, Baldassare (1478–1529). *The Courtier.* Trans. George Bull. New York: Viking Penguin, 1967.

Elyot, Thomas (1490–1546). *Defence of Good Women: The Feminist Controversy of the Renaissance.* Ed. Diane Bornstein. Facsimile. New York: Delmar, 1980.

Erasmus, Desiderius (1467–1536). "Courtship," "The Girl with No Interest in Marriage," "The Repentant Girl," "Marriage," "The Abbot and the Learned Lady," and

"The New Mother." In *The Colloquies of Erasmus*, trans. Craig R. Thompson, pp. 88–98, 99–111, 111–14, 114–27, 217–23. Chicago: University of Chicago Press, 1965.

Kempe, Margery (1373–1439). *The Book of Margery Kempe*. Trans. Barry Windeatt. New York: Viking Penguin, 1986.

King, Margaret L., and Albert Rabil, Jr., eds. *Her Immaculate Hand: Selected Works by and about the Women Humanists of Quattrocento Italy*. 2d rev. ed. Binghamton, N.Y.: Medieval and Renaissance Texts and Studies, 1991.

Klein, Joan Larsen, ed. *Daughters, Wives, and Widows: Writings by Men about Women and Marriage in England, 1500–1640*. Urbana: University of Illinois Press, 1992.

Knox, John (1505–72). *The Political Writings of John Knox: The First Blast of the Trumpet against the Monstrous Regiment of Women and Other Selected Works*. Ed. Marvin A. Breslow. Washington, D.C.: Folger Shakespeare Library, 1985.

Kors, Alan C., and Edward Peters, eds. *Witchcraft in Europe, 1100–1700: A Documentary History*. Philadelphia: University of Pennsylvania Press, 1972.

Krämer, Heinrich, and Jacob Sprenger. *Malleus Maleficarum* (c. 1487). Trans. Montague Summers. London: Pushkin Press, 1928; rpt., New York: Dover, 1971. The "Hammer of Witches," a convenient source for all the misogynistic commonplaces on the eve of the sixteenth century, and an important text in the witch craze of the following centuries.

Lorris, Guillaume de, and Jean de Meun. *The Romance of the Rose*. Trans. Charles Dahlbert. Princeton: Princeton University Press, 1971; rpt., Hanover, N.H.: University Press of New England, 1983.

Navarre, Marguerite de (1492–1549). *The Heptameron*. Trans. P. A. Chilton. New York: Viking Penguin, 1984.

Pizan, Christine de (1365–1431). *The Book of the City of Ladies*. Trans. Earl Jeffrey Richards; foreword Marina Warner. New York: Persea Books, 1982.

———. *The Treasure of the City of Ladies or, The Book of The Three Virtues*. Trans. Sarah Lawson. New York: Viking Penguin, 1985.

———. *A Medieval Woman's Mirror of Honor: The Treasury of the City of Ladies*. Trans. and introd. Charity Cannon Willard; ed. and introd. Madeleine P. Cosman. New York: Persea Books, 1989.

Spenser, Edmund (1552–99). *The Faerie Queene*. Ed. Thomas P. Roche, Jr., with assistance of C. Patrick O'Donnell, Jr. New Haven: Yale University Press, 1978.

Teresa of Avila, St. (1515–82). *The Life of Saint Teresa of Avila by Herself*. Trans. J. M. Cohen. New York: Viking Penguin, 1957.

Vives, Juan Luis (1492–1540). *The Instruction of the Christian Woman*. Trans. Rycharde Hyrde. London, 1524, 1557.

Weyer, Johann (1515–88). *Witches, Devils, and Doctors in the Renaissance: Johann Weyer, "De praestigiis daemonum."* Ed. George Mora with Benjamin G. Kohl, Erik Midelfort, and Helen Bacon; trans. John Shea. Binghamton, N.Y.: Medieval and Renaissance Texts and Studies, 1991.

Wilson, Katharina M., ed. *Medieval Women Writers*. Athens: University of Georgia Press, 1984.

———. *Women Writers of the Renaissance and Reformation*. Athens: University of Georgia Press, 1987.

Wilson, Katharina M., and Frank J. Warnke, eds. *Women Writers of the Seventeenth Century*. Athens: University of Georgia Press, 1989.

SECONDARY WORKS

The Misogynist Tradition

Bloch, R. Howard. *Medieval Misogyny and the Invention of Western Romantic Love.* Chicago: University of Chicago Press, 1991.

Clark, Elizabeth A. *Ascetic Piety and Women's Faith: Essays on Late Ancient Christianity.* Lewiston, N.Y.: Edwin Mellen Press, 1986.

Dixon, Suzanne. *The Roman Family.* Baltimore: Johns Hopkins University Press, 1992.

Gardner, Jane F. *Women in Roman Law and Society.* Bloomington: Indiana University Press, 1986.

Horowitz, Maryanne Cline. "Aristotle and Women." *Journal of the History of Biology* 9 (1976): 183–213.

Lochrie, Karma. *Margery Kempe and Translations of the Flesh.* Philadelphia: University of Pennsylvania Press, 1992.

Maclean, Ian. *The Renaissance Notion of Women: A Study of the Fortunes of Scholasticism and Medical Science in European Intellectual Life.* Cambridge: Cambridge University Press, 1980.

Okin, Susan Moller. *Women in Western Political Thought.* Princeton: Princeton University Press, 1979.

Pagels, Elaine. *Adam, Eve, and the Serpent.* New York: Harper Collins, 1988.

Pomeroy, Sarah B. *Goddesses, Whores, Wives, and Slaves: Women in Classical Antiquity.* New York: Schocken Books, 1976.

Tetel, Marcel. *Marguerite de Navarre's Heptameron: Themes, Language, and Structure.* Durham, N.C.: Duke University Press, 1973.

Treggiari, Susan. *Roman Marriage: Iusti Coniuges from the Time of Cicero to the Time of Ulpian.* Oxford: Oxford University Press, 1991.

Walsh, William T. *St. Teresa of Avila: A Biography.* Rockford, Ill.: TAN Books and Publications, 1987.

Warner, Marina. *Alone of All Her Sex: The Myth and Cult of the Virgin Mary.* New York: Knopf, 1976.

The Other Voice

Beilin, Elaine V. *Redeeming Eve: Women Writers of the English Renaissance.* Princeton: Princeton University Press, 1987.

Benson, Pamela Joseph. *The Invention of Renaissance Woman: The Challenge of Female Independence in the Literature and Thought of Italy and England.* University Park: Pennsylvania State University Press, 1992.

Davis, Natalie Zemon. *Society and Culture in Early Modern France.* Stanford: Stanford University Press, 1975.

Davis, Natalie Zemon, and Arlette Farge, eds. *Renaissance and Enlightenment Paradoxes.* Vol. 3 of *A History of Women in the West.* Cambridge, Mass.: Harvard University Press, 1993.

Ferguson, Margaret W., Maureen Quilligan, and Nancy J. Vickers, eds. *Rewriting the Renaissance: The Discourses of Sexual Difference in Early Modern Europe.* Chicago: University of Chicago Press, 1987.

Herlihy, David. "Did Women Have a Renaissance? A Reconsideration." *Medievalia et Humanistica,* n. s. 13 (1985): 1–22.

Hull, Suzanne W. *Chaste, Silent, and Obedient: English Books for Women, 1475–1640.* San Marino, Calif.: Huntington Library, 1982.

Jordan, Constance. *Renaissance Feminism: Literary Texts and Political Models.* Ithaca: Cornell University Press, 1990.

Kelly, Joan. "Did Women Have a Renaissance?" In *Women, History, and Theory,* pp. 19–50. Chicago: University of Chicago Press, 1984. Reprinted in *Becoming Visible: Women in European History,* ed. Renate Bridenthal, Claudia Koonz, and Susan M. Stuard, pp. 175–202. 2d ed. Boston: Houghton Mifflin, 1987.

———. "Early Feminist Theory and the *Querelle des Femmes.*" In *Women, History, and Theory.* Chicago: University of Chicago Press, 1984.

Kelso, Ruth. *Doctrine for the Lady of the Renaissance.* Foreword by Katharine M. Rogers. Urbana: University of Illinois Press, 1956, 1978.

King, Margaret L. *Women of the Renaissance.* Foreword by Catharine R. Stimpson. Chicago: University of Chicago Press, 1991.

Klapisch-Zuber, Christiane, ed. *Silences of the Middle Ages.* Vol. 2 of *A History of Women in the West.* Cambridge, Mass.: Harvard University Press, 1992.

Laqueur, Thomas. *Making Sex: Body and Gender from the Greeks to Freud.* Cambridge, Mass.: Harvard University Press, 1990.

Lerner, Gerda. *Creation of Feminist Consciousness, 1000–1870.* New York: Oxford University Press, 1994.

Maclean, Ian. *Woman Triumphant: Feminism in French Literature, 1610–1652.* Oxford: Clarendon Press, 1977.

Matter, E. Ann, and John Coakley, eds. *Creative Women in Medieval and Early Modern Italy.* Philadelphia: University of Pennsylvania Press, 1994.

Monson, Craig A., ed. *The Crannied Wall: Women, Religion, and the Arts in Early Modern Europe.* Ann Arbor: University of Michigan Press, 1992.

Pantel, Pauline Schmitt, ed. *From Ancient Goddesses to Christian Saints.* Vol. 1 of *A History of Women in the West.* Cambridge, Mass.: Harvard University Press, 1992.

Rose, Mary Beth, ed. *Women in the Middle Ages and the Renaissance: Literary and Historical Perspectives.* Syracuse: Syracuse University Press, 1986.

Stuard, Susan M. "The Dominion of Gender: Women's Fortunes in the High Middle Ages." In *Becoming Visible: Women in European History,* ed. Renate Bridenthal, Claudia Koonz, and Susan M. Stuard, pp. 153–72. 2d ed. Boston: Houghton Mifflin, 1987.

Wiesner, Merry E. *Women and Gender in Early Modern Europe.* Cambridge: Cambridge University Press, 1993.

Willard, Charity Cannon. *Christine de Pizan: Her Life and Works.* New York: Persea Books, 1984.

Wilson, Katharina, ed. *An Encyclopedia of Continental Women Writers.* New York: Garland, 1991.

Power and Obedience

Matter, E. Ann, and John Coakley, eds. *Creative Women in Medieval and Early Modern Italy: A Religious and Artistic Renaissance.* Philadelphia: University of Pennsylvania Press, 1994.

Monson, Craig A., ed. *The Crannied Wall: Women, Religion, and the Arts in Early Modern Europe.* Ann Arbor: University of Michigan Press, 1992.

Zarri, Gabriella. "Living Saints: A Typology of Female Sanctity in the Early Sixteenth Century," trans. Daniel Bornstein. In *Women and Religion in Medieval and Renaissance Italy*, ed. Daniel Bornstein and Roberto Rusconi, pp. 219–302. Chicago:
University of Chicago Press, 1996.

Pretense

Bell, Rudolph M. *Holy Anorexia.* Chicago: University of Chicago Press, 1985.
Brown, Judith C. *Immodest Acts: The Life of a Lesbian Nun in Renaissance Italy.* New York:
Oxford University Press, 1986.
Ciammitti, Luisa. "One Saint Less: The Story of Angela Mellini, Bolognese Seam-
stress (1667–17[?])." In *Sex and Gender in Historical Perspective: Selections from "Quaderni
Storici"*, ed. Edward Muir and Guido Ruggiero, pp. 141–76. Baltimore: Johns
Hopkins University Press, 1990.
Davis, Natalie Zemon. *The Return of Martin Guerre.* Cambridge, Mass.: Harvard Uni-
versity Press, 1983.
Henningsen, Gustav. *The Witches' Advocate: Basque Witchcraft and the Spanish Inquisition
(1609–1614).* Reno: University of Nevada Press, 1980.
Perry, Mary Elizabeth. "Beatas and the Inquisition in Early Modern Spain." In *Inquisi-
tion and Society in Early Modern Europe*, ed. Stephen Haliczer, pp. 147–68. London:
Croom Helm, and New York: Barnes and Noble, 1987.
Schutte, Anne Jacobson. "Discernment and Discipline: Giorgio Polacco and Reli-
gious Women in Early Modern Italy." In *Culture and Self in Renaissance Europe*, ed.
William J. Connell. Berkeley: University of California Press, forthcoming.
———. "'Questo non è il ritratto che ho fatto io': Painters, the Inquisition, and the
Shape of Sanctity in Seventeenth-Century Venice." In *Florence and Italy: Studies in
Honour of Nicolai Rubinstein*, ed. Peter Denley and Caroline Elam, pp. 419–31. Lon-
don: Westfield College, 1988.
Tomizza, Fulvio. *Heavenly Supper: The Story of Maria Janis.* Trans. Anne Jacobson
Schutte. Chicago: University of Chicago Press, 1991.
Weinstein, Donald, and Rudolph Bell. *Saints and Society: The Two Worlds of Western Chris-
tendom, 1000–1700.* Chicago: University of Chicago Press, 1982.
Zagorin, Perez. *Ways of Lying: Dissimulation, Persecution, and Conformity in Early Modern
Europe.* Cambridge, Mass.: Harvard University Press, 1990.

Purity and Danger

Cohen, Elizabeth S. "No Longer Virgins: Self-Representation by Young Women in
Late Renaissance Rome." In *Refiguring Woman: Perspectives on Gender and the Italian
Renaissance*, ed. Marilyn Migiel and Juliana Schiesari, pp. 169–91. Ithaca: Cornell
University Press, 1991.
Cohen, Sherrill. *The Evolution of Women's Asylums since 1500: From Refuges for Ex-Prostitutes
to Shelters for Battered Women.* New York: Oxford University Press, 1992.
Ferrante, Lucia. "Honor Regained: Women in the Casa del Soccorso di San Paolo in
Sixteenth-Century Bologna." In *Sex and Gender in Historical Perspective: Selections from
"Quaderni Storici"*, ed. Edward Muir and Guido Ruggiero, pp. 46–72. Baltimore:
Johns Hopkins University Press, 1990.
Pullan, Brian. *Rich and Poor in Renaissance Venice: The Social Institutions of a Catholic State, to
1605.* Oxford: Basil Blackwell, 1971.

Zarri, Gabriella. "Ursula and Catherine: The Marriage of Virgins in the Sixteenth Century," trans. Anne Jacobson Schutte. In *Creative Women in Medieval and Early Modern Italy: A Religious and Artistic Renaissance,* ed. E. Ann Matter and John Coakley, pp. 237–78. Philadelphia: University of Pennsylvania Press, 1994.

The Roman Inquisition and Venice
Ginzburg, Carlo. "The Inquisitor as Anthropologist." In *Clues, Myths, and the Historical Method,* trans. John Tedeschi and Anne C. Tedeschi, pp. 156–64. Baltimore: Johns Hopkins University Press, 1989.
Grendler, Paul F. *The Roman Inquisition and the Venetian Press, 1540–1605.* Princeton: Princeton University Press, 1977.
Martin, John. "Out of the Shadow: Heretical and Catholic Women in Renaissance Venice." *Journal of Family History* 10 (1985): 21–33.
———. *Venice's Hidden Enemies: Italian Heretics in a Renaissance City.* Berkeley: University of California Press, 1993.
Martin, Ruth. *Witchcraft and the Inquisition in Venice, 1550–1650.* Oxford: Basil Blackwell, 1989.
Tedeschi, John. *The Prosecution of Heresy: Collected Studies on the Inquisition in Early Modern Italy.* Binghamton, N.Y.: Medieval and Renaissance Texts and Studies, 1991.
———. "The Status of the Defendant before the Roman Inquisition." In *Ketzerverfolgung im 16. und frühen 17. Jahrhundert,* ed. Hans Rudolf Guggisberg, Bernd Moeller, and Silvana Seidel Menchi, pp. 125–46. Wiesbaden: Harrassowitz, 1992.

Writing and Speaking
Davis, Natalie Zemon. "Boundaries and the Sense of Self in Sixteenth-Century France." In *Reconstructing Individualism: Autonomy, Individualism, and the Self in Western Thought,* ed. Thomas C. Heller, Morton Sosna, and David E. Wellbery, pp. 53–63. Stanford: Stanford University Press, 1986.
———. *Fiction in the Archives: Pardon Tales and Their Tellers in Sixteenth-Century France.* Stanford: Stanford University Press, 1987.
———. *Women on the Margins: Three Seventeenth-Century Lives.* Cambridge, Mass.: Harvard University Press, 1995.
Reay, Barry. "The Context and Meaning of Popular Literacy: Some Evidence from Nineteenth-Century Rural England." *Past and Present* 131 (May 1991): 89–129.
Schutte, Anne Jacobson. "Inquisition and Female Autobiography: The Case of Cecilia Ferrazzi." In *The Crannied Wall: Women, Religion, and the Arts in Early Modern Europe,* ed. Craig A. Monson, pp. 105–18. Ann Arbor: University of Michigan Press, 1992.
———. "Per Speculum in Enigmate: Failed Saints, Artists, and Self-Construction of the Female Body in Early Modern Italy." In *Creative Women in Medieval and Early Modern Italy: A Religious and Artistic Renaissance,* ed. E. Ann Matter and John Coakley, pp. 188–200. Philadelphia: University of Pennsylvania Press, 1994.
Stanton, Domna C., ed. *The Female Autograph: Theory and Practice of Autobiography from the Tenth to the Twentieth Century.* Chicago: University of Chicago Press, 1987.
Weber, Alison. *Teresa of Avila and the Rhetoric of Femininity.* Princeton: Princeton University Press, 1990.

INDEX